# STUDIES IN ENGLISH LITERATURE No. 70

*General Editor*
David Daiches

## Already published in the series:

# Already published in the series *(continued)*:

# BEOWULF

by

## T. A. SHIPPEY
*Fellow of St John's College, Oxford*

EDWARD ARNOLD

First published 1978 by
Edward Arnold (Publishers) Ltd
41 Bedford Square
London WC1B 3DP

ISBN 0 7131 6147 7 Boards
ISBN 0 7131 6148 5 Paper

*Acknowledgement:* The poem is quoted with line references, and reprinted by permission of the publisher, from *Beowulf*, ed. F. Klaeber (3rd edn, Lexington, Mass.: D. C. Heath and Company, 1950). Editorial diacritics have not been reproduced.

*Printed and bound in Great Britain at*
*The Camelot Press Ltd, Southampton*

# General Preface

The object of this series is to provide studies of individual novels, plays and groups of poems and essays which are known to be widely read by students. The emphasis is on clarification and evaluation; biographical and historical facts, while they may be discussed when they throw light on particular elements in a writer's work, are generally subordinated to critical discussion. What kind of work is this? What exactly goes on here? How good is this work, and why? These are the questions that each writer will try to answer.

It should be emphasized that these studies are written on the assumption that the reader has already read carefully the work discussed. The objective is not to enable students to deliver opinions about works they have not read, nor is it to provide ready-made ideas to be applied to works that have been read. In one sense all critical interpretation can be regarded as foisting opinions on readers, but to accept this is to deny the advantages of any sort of critical discussion directed at students or indeed at anybody else. The aim of these studies is to provide what Coleridge called in another context 'aids to reflection' about the works discussed. The interpretations are offered as suggestive rather than as definitive, in the hope of stimulating the reader into developing further his own insights. This is after all the function of all critical discourse among sensible people.

Because of the interest which this kind of study has aroused, it has been decided to extend it first from merely English literature to include also some selected works of American literature and now further to include selected works in English by Commonwealth writers. The criterion will remain that the book studied is important in itself and is widely read by students.

DAVID DAICHES

# Contents

# 1. Introduction

Criticism of *Beowulf* began in falsity and bias. In 1705 Humfrey Wanley wrote that in the poem *descripta videntur bella, quae Beowulfus (quidam Danus ex Regia Scyldingorum stirpe ortus) gessit contra Sueciae Regulos* [are seen described the wars which Beowulf (a certain Dane sprung from the royal stock of the Scyldings) waged against the petty kings of Sweden]. All the facts given by this précis are wrong. The hero of the poem was not a Dane nor a Scylding, and though he did wage war against the Swedes, the poet's account of them occupies only six lines (2391–6) out of more than three thousand. Wanley was misled by the fact that there are two Beowulfs in the poem, but more seriously by his underlying assumption that epics ought to be about 'arms and the man', about the foundation of dynasties and the warlike birth of nations. Grímur Thorkelin, the Icelander who published the first printed edition of *Beowulf* in 1815, knew enough to correct Wanley on the point of the hero's nationality, but still felt obliged to insist that the poem was *de Danorum Rebus Gestis* [about the deeds of the Danes], that it was a *Scyldingid* comparable with Homer's *Iliad* and Virgil's *Aeneid*.

These errors of antiquity were not, perhaps, inevitable, but they have remained typical. All critics of *Beowulf* feel the temptation, at some point, to assimilate the poem to contemporary canons of 'good taste', whether these are neo-classical and nationalistic, as in Thorkelin's time, or socially conscious and morally concerned, as in the present day. Partly this is because the poem is defenceless: we do not know when it was written, or how, by whom, or for what kind of audience. It is accordingly easy to fit 'backgrounds' to it and insist that these must dominate interpretation. However, the consistency of critical uneasiness over the centuries suggests that there is also in the poem something deeply if accidentally provocative. It is this which made Brigid Brophy and her colleagues put it first on their list of *Fifty Works of Literature We Can Do Without*, which calls forth the traditional undergraduate jokes about mead-swilling and retarded ceorls, and which led Kingsley Amis to write his itch-scratching poem:

So, bored with dragons, he lay down to sleep,
Locking for good his massive hoard of words . . .

The common factor in all these snipings, one should note, is embarrass-
ment. Again and again *Beowulf* produces in readers (especially highly
trained readers) that feeling which simple people experience the first time
they see Frenchmen kissing each other formally and in public – surprise,
horror, a dumb sense that social signals no longer mean what they
should. The simplest way of coping with this is to laugh, so that the taboo
is acceptably transformed into the comic. A politer means of evasion is to
look the other way. Truth, however, depends on grasping the fact that
social signals are arbitrary, conventional and to be understood only within
the system of which they are part. Without this all-purpose insight
*Beowulf* remains incomprehensible, at the mercy of critical fashion.

Take, for instance, boasting. Our own culture puts very strong
emphasis on modest self-deprecation: it is in all circumstances wrong to
speak of oneself highly and without qualification. This embargo is
reinforced by such literary stereotypes as the 'braggart soldier' of
Spenser or Shakespeare, whose words mask his cowardice, or the 'strong,
silent Englishman' of popular fiction fifty years ago (his silence, note,
was an index of his strength). But *Beowulf* ignores it. Before every major
combat its hero delivers at least one speech in praise of his own courage,
promising to do great deeds (632–8), to pursue Grendel's mother
wherever she may hide (1392–4), not to flee from the dragon the space of
a foot (2524–7). On this last occasion he goes further and orders his men
not to accompany him: 'It is no expedition for you, nor is it in the power
of any man but me alone that he should try his strength with the monster,
perform heroic deeds' (2532–5). He turns out to be wrong here (one of his
men comes to save him), and critics have found the boast hard to forgive.
Yet other characters in the poem appreciate and admire his speeches; we
are told of the Danish queen:

> Ðam wife þa word      wel licodon,
> gilpcwide Geates.                              (639–40)

[The words pleased the woman greatly, the boasting speech of the
Geat.]

Our difficulties are summed up in the word *gilp*, used thirteen times in
*Beowulf* and for the most part favourably, but surviving in modern
English only as 'yelp', the ignominious and empty noise of curs. Semantic
and cultural shifts like that make it hard to view Beowulf impartially and,
in particular, to observe that, though his limits on boastfulness are not

ours, nevertheless he does observe one limit very strictly. In all his *gylpspraece* he never promises success. He promises to succeed *or die* (see lines 636–7, 1490–91, 2535–7). The striking similarity of these three speech-endings suggests that men in the Beowulfian culture knew a brag from a promise as well as we do, but that they were allowed to feel confident in their own will-power as we are not – a difference, certainly, but not a ridiculous one.

A fair response to *Beowulf* therefore involves a relative view of modesty. The same is true of drink. Ale, beer, wine and mead are mentioned more than forty times in the poem, while there is no word for any item of food at all – the source, evidently, of many modern objections. Worse still, the characters view this with complacency. When Beowulf says to Unferth that he has said a great deal about Breca, *beore druncen* (531), he clearly means that Unferth is 'drunk on beer' and accordingly unreliable. The Danish queen Wealhtheow, however, once more causes semantic difficulty when she uses the same word in her idyllic description of Heorot (1228–31): 'Here every man is true to the other, kind-hearted and loyal to his lord, the thanes are united, the people all willing, the drunken retainers [*druncne dryhtguman*] do as I say.' Nervousness breaks out among many translators at this stage, with *druncne* rendered as 'carousing' or 'cheered with drink' or 'wine-glad' or even more circuitous paraphrase. But the problem is a cultural one; we cannot translate *druncne* as 'drunken' only because it seems to us not to collocate with words like 'true' and 'loyal' and 'united'. Our conventional wisdom says that drunkenness is associated with weakness of character.

One result is that we find it hard to respond to the willed evocation of warmth and joviality in such scenes as the one Beowulf imagines in lines 603–6:

> 'Gæþ eft se þe mot
> to medo modig,      siþþan morgenleoht
> ofer ylda bearn      oþres dogores,
> sunne sweglwered      suþan scineð!'

[He who can will then go boldly to his mead, once the light of next day's morning, the sun clothed in glory, shines from the south over the children of men.]

To us strong drink and early morning cheerfulness are proverbially opposed. However, there are more serious consequences of the old English/modern English cultural gap, centring for the most part on the problem of violence.

This most powerful of modern impieties is now generally reclassified as 'obscene', while it is axiomatic that 'violence breeds violence' and 'violence never solves anything'. The story of *Beowulf*, though, rests on three sudden applications of force, which are largely successful. In so far as they are not, moreover, one might conclude that the weakness stems from an insufficiency of violence rather than an excess of it; if Beowulf had been stronger and better supported he might even have survived the dragon. In any case the main and distinctive quality of the hero is not his courtesy nor his piety nor even his courage, but his physical strength (which we are very likely to call 'raw' or 'brute'). The poet furthermore relishes disturbingly his many opportunities for describing violence, and exploits them in a direct and earthy way. When Beowulf seizes Grendel's hand *fingras burston* [fingers burst], *seonowe onsprungon, burston banlocan* [sinews sprang, bone-locks burst]. As the giant sword cuts through Grendel's mother's neck, the poet is there to explore the shearing process:

> banhringas bræc;    bil eal ðurhwod
> fægne flæschoman;   heo on flet gecrong,
> sweord wæs swatig,   secg weorce gefeh.   (1567–9)

[It broke the bone-rings; the sword drove right through the doomed covering of flesh. She fell to the floor. The sword was bloody, the man rejoiced in his deed.]

'Bone-ring' is an expressive and realistic coinage for 'vertebra'; one feels it was not only Beowulf who rejoiced in the blood and bone and flesh. And if one thinks reassuringly that these actions are after all carried out only against cannibalistic monsters, who themselves drink blood, snap joints, devour feet and hands like man-eating tigers, it is worth recalling 'Dayraven', the Frankish standard-bearer whom Beowulf remembers killing near the end of his own life – a man, be it noted, fighting in defence of his own home. He did not die by the sword, Beowulf ruminates:

> 'ac him hildegrap    heortan wylmas,
> banhus gebræc.'                              (2507–8)

[But my war-grip broke his bone-house and the pulses of his heart.]

The smashed ribs, the squeezed heart once more make Beowulf's bear-hug tactile. The poet is, in fact, taking evident aesthetic pleasure in the details of violence.

Here many critics dig in their heels. Morality insists that ferocity must not pay. The poet is only 'bringing the realities of violence home', illustrating graphically the impulse which leads all heroes to their deaths.

Such arguments can be pressed forcefully; they look, however, like a new form of 'bowdlerization'. It is better to grasp the nettle at once and admit that, as with drink and boasting, violence played a different part in the poet's culture from that which it does in ours. Yet a final conclusion may be that no matter how many allowances are made for cultural gaps and semantic shifts, one more will always turn out to be vital. Since literary training and common experience are such poor guides to the poet's assumptions, how can anyone hope to interpret such fleeting matters as tone of voice, shade of meaning, reliable or unreliable narration?

The answer to this lies in the modern demonstration that any text, prose or poetry, carries much more information within it than its creator realized or intended. What was implicit knowledge for the poet and his Anglo-Saxon audience may need to be made explicit for us, and the possibility that one's judgements are ethnocentric has always to be reckoned with. Just the same, many of the poet's beliefs and prejudices are downright familiar, and others respond to analysis. The essential caveat is that the framework within which judgements are made needs to be set up before fine literary details are filled in. Good readers have probably always done this, consciously or unconsciously; bad readers have approached the poem already burdened with their own hypothetical *Scyldingids*.

# 2. The World of the Poem

## Words and meaning

A single scene will do to document these assertions – that of Beowulf's arrival in Denmark and his challenge by the coastguard (lines 229–300), a scene which turns on an evident if unacknowledged crux. What has happened so far is that we have been introduced to the Danish royal dynasty, the Scyldings; have seen the present king, Hrothgar, build the great hall of Heorot; and have then been told how Grendel, 'the mighty spirit', haunts it and kills its inhabitants. The news reaches Beowulf, still named only as 'Hygelac's thane'; he chooses his men and sets sail for Denmark. But as soon as he arrives, this speedy progress is checked by the Danish coastguard, who rides down and, in the poem's first passage of direct speech, asks the hero who he is. Beowulf replies, still without revealing his name, but giving his father's and stating his business. The coastguard then begins his next speech with a brief maxim or aphorism:

> 'Æghwæþres sceal
> scearp scyldwiga      gescad witan,
> worda ond worca,      se þe wel þenceð.'      (287–9)

Translating this ought not to be difficult. *Æghwæþer* can mean 'each' or 'every', and *gescad* comes from a root meaning to divide, or separate, or decide, so there is a little semantic play in the concepts, but hardly very much. The latest published rendering (Howell D. Chickering's text and translation of 1977) has: 'A keen-witted shield-bearer who thinks things out carefully must know the distinction between words and deeds, keep the difference clear.' This is syntactically accurate. However, it makes no sense. Any fool can tell the difference between words and deeds, and Beowulf's deeds anyway turn out much the same as his words. What can the coastguard mean?

The problem here is caused by the fact that proverbs are not merely linguistic phenomena. We know this from our own experience, since we habitually use formulas which are entirely tautologous ('Business is business') or on a literal level meaningless ('Don't cross your bridges till you come to them'), without feeling any block in communication at all.

The hidden factor is the extra-linguistic frame; we have been taught in childhood when to use proverbs, what their metaphors mean, who to say them to, and how to take them. It is this non-verbal knowledge that we need to be able to understand the coastguard's 'gnome'. Reluctance to reconstruct such intangibles and dogged staring at 'the text' have led literary critics only into controversy. Thus one scholar decided that the words were just a pompous way for the coastguard to say he was a keen-witted shield-bearer; another thought they were a kind of apology; a third takes them as grudging deference ('I suppose you know what you are talking about'); naturally they have been seen as conveying involved and subtle moral lessons.[1] In fact the answer is not especially obscure; but to reach it one must consider not the maxim alone, but the maxim in social and dramatic context.

Strong clues to its purport have already been given by the cautious balancing of both the coastguard's initial challenge and Beowulf's subsequent reply. Superficially the coastguard is threatening: he does not dismount, he waves a spear, the first thing he says is 'Who are you?' The *second* thing he says, though, is his job: 'I have long been the frontier-guard, kept watch over the sea. . . .' So his questions are not idle or unofficial. He goes on to state the reasons why he ought to be suspicious, and also why his suspicions might be allayed: Beowulf and his men have come openly and without permission (innocence or defiance?), one of them is of imposing physique and appearance (danger or reassurance?). Only after these balanced clauses does he repeat his demand to know who the intruders are, and then he does it with possibly studied impersonality: 'haste is best', he says, not 'you had better hurry.'

In his speech one might well feel that, <u>though no threat has been expressed, there is one</u> somewhere nearby. That seems exactly what the situation calls for. The coastguard is prepared to use words like 'pirates' and 'spies' [*scipherge, leassceaweras*], and recognizes that even Beowulf's noble bearing may belie him. Violence therefore remains a necessary option. At the same time he keeps these potential insults in the subjunctive, not applying them openly till the chance of peace has been ruled out. Tact and firmness are the Dane's most evident qualities. To this Beowulf replies with something like submissiveness, though not apology: he explains his business, but twice invites the coastguard to correct him if he has been misinformed – 'give us good advice' (269),

[1] For these opinions see, respectively, W. S. Mackie, *Modern Language Review* 34 (1939), p. 517; F. Klaeber's edition, *op. cit.*, p. 139; James Smith, *English* 25 (1976), p. 227; M. Pepperdene, 'Beowulf and the Coastguard', *English Studies* 47 (1966), pp. 409–19.

'you will know if things are indeed as we have heard said' (272–3). When he declares his intention of helping the Danes to fight Grendel, he does so for once with reasonable humility, spending six lines on the possibility that he will fail. Beowulf and the coastguard, in short, make signals to each other of mutual respect, taking care to adopt the appropriate roles of Official Inspector (not Personal Challenger), Modest Petitioner (rather than Officious Volunteer). The question of dominance is not raised. Both speeches exude the wary politeness of a society in which men habitually go armed.

And then the coastguard has to make up his mind, which he does immediately after quoting his maxim. Yet the situation *has not changed*. The newcomers have no passports; though one of them has spoken nicely it is without corroboration; the risk of piracy must still be there. In this context the two lines of traditional saying express two different awarenesses – one, that doubt remains, for words are all that have passed, and 'deeds speak louder than words'; that just the same decision cannot be shirked, for 'needs must when the devil drives'. It is the duty of a sharp shield-warrior to decide correctly, even on inadequate evidence. 'He must be able to judge *everything*, words *as well as* deeds.' That is what the maxim says, and the coastguard follows it immediately by doing the right thing and letting the newcomers pass with a firmly 'performative' verb, '*Ic þæt gehyre* . . .', 'I hear that this warband is friendly to the lord of the Danes.' He backs his judgement to the length of allowing them to keep their weapons and offering to look after their boat.

The scene and the saying form an excellent example of heroic good manners. Naturally we need to adjust our socially determined notions of politeness to understand both properly. It is hard to resist the conclusion, furthermore, that the poet was appealing to a taste already formed. The exchanges with the coastguard and Wulfgar the doorward immediately following are, after all, redundant to the story as a whole; we could have been taken to the intersection between Beowulf and Heorot much more briskly. Their inclusion suggests that the poet knew his audience would relish displays of oral and aural skills from the characters, and would also expect to use such skills themselves (for the coastguard's saying is true generally as well as in context, and could be taken as warning listeners to weigh words wisely too).

However, the main difficulty they present for readers brought up on novels is that they are overwhelmingly 'superficial': meaning has to be decoded from words and deeds alone (just as in real life), with only the slightest indications of *thought*. One may well wonder whether this is true of *Beowulf* all the time. Is there any sense in it of discrepancy between the inner character and the outer social role?

## Characters and emotions

One can see straight away that the poet has a sharp eye for discrepancy between actions and feelings. After Beowulf has made his boast that he will fight weaponless against Grendel, he disarms and lies down to sleep in Heorot. In a tableau of heroic propriety his thanes follow suit, surrounding their lord in sleep as they ought to in battle: 'around him many a bold sea-warrior turned to his bed in the hall' (689–90). But with the image established, the poet instantly penetrates it:

> Nænig heora þohte,     þæt he þanon scolde
> eft eardlufan     æfre gesecean,
> folc oþðe freoburh,     þær he afeded wæs;
> ac hie hæfdon gefrunen,     þæt hie ær to fela micles
> in þæm winsele     wældeað fornam,
> Denigea leode.                              (691–6)

[Not one of them thought that he would ever leave again in search of his loved home, the noble place and people where he was brought up; but they had heard that in that winehall violent death had taken far too many of the Danish people.]

His aside does not shatter the tableau, but adds to it a silent stoicism. Still, it shows the poet recognizing that his characters *have* feelings. Does he, however, possess the vocabulary to take inner analysis much further? There are examples which suggest that he has not.

The only things we are told directly about the coastguard's state of mind, for instance, are that he was unafraid (287), and actuated by curiosity (232). When he saw the shields and armour coming over the gangplank, *hine fyrwyt bræc* . . . , 'curiosity urged him in his thoughts, what these men were'. But this phrase is used twice more in the poem, once in line 1985, when Beowulf's king Hygelac asks him how he coped with Grendel – 'curiosity urged him' [*hyne fyrwet bræc*] – and once in line 2784. This follows the death of the dragon, when Wiglaf robs its treasures and takes them back to the dying Beowulf, so he can leave life easier:

> Ar wæs on ofoste,     eftsiðes georn,
> frætwum gefyrðred;     hyne fyrwet bræc,
> hwæðer collenferð     cwicne gemette.     (2783–5)

[The messenger was in haste, eager to get back, speeded by his treasures; curiosity urged him, whether the bold man would find (Beowulf) alive.]

'Curiosity' seems a callous word here. 'Anxiety' would be better, but that would not fit the completely relaxed enquiry of Hygelac, or even the tense but fearless figure of the coastguard. The poet is using one word to cover mental states we would think perceptibly different – a habit which occasionally leads to deeper confusion.

*Hreow*, for example, is the Old English ancestor of 'rue', and normally has associations of regret or penitence. In *Beowulf*, though, it is used once to describe Hrothgar's reaction to the killing of Æschere by Grendel's mother (2129), and once of Beowulf's reaction to the dragon burning his hall (2328). In both cases it is hard to see how 'distress' can be taken as far as 'penitence', and there is a suspicion that the poet cannot distinguish *hreow* from the etymologically unconnected adjective *hreoh*, 'fierce, disturbed', a word used repeatedly by itself and in compounds to describe the very similar mixture of anger and pain felt by kings and heroes and monsters when they are hurt (see lines 1307, 2132, 2296, etc.). In any case the poet uses *wælreow*, 'fierce and deadly', with evident approbation at line 629, *blodreow*, 'fierce and bloody', with equally evident dislike in line 1719. The semantic field of *hreow/hreoh* between them seems too broad for exactness, while there is equally little useful distinction between any of the poet's frequent words for 'sad' and 'sorrow' – *wræc*, *torn*, *brecð*, and the rest. Characters' feelings are intense, for they 'burn' and 'boil' and 'seethe'; but they are not sharply discriminated.

Yet there are half a dozen places in the poem where we are asked to dwell on complex mental progressions, some of them seemingly close to the story's central theme. Many critics feel that the speech of Hrothgar between lines 1700 and 1784 encapsulates the moral of the poem, and its centre is in turn an account of a sinner's development. For some eleven lines Hrothgar describes the root of sin in success, in the physical happiness and freedom of a lucky man, like Beowulf. The result, he says, is that:

> 'he þæt wyrse ne con – ,
> oð þæt him on innan      oferhygda dæl
> weaxeð ond wridað.'                                    (1739–41)

[He does not know the worse – till inside him great arrogance grows and spreads.]

And having said so much Hrothgar moves rapidly on to allegory – the guardian of the soul, the enemy nearby shooting his arrows, the sinner overcome by diabolic promptings. The 'rake's progress' continues with a picture of avarice and envy, visible results of inner failure. But what *was* the inner failure? Are arrogance and prosperity *inevitably* connected?

What is 'the worse', and what the 'bitter arrow' that strikes the sleeping soul? Modern criticism is naturally drawn to explicate these questions, and we would like very much to know as well why Beowulf makes no reply to the whole speech, and whether he sees any connection between it and the calamity which falls on him at the end of his days. When the dragon comes, is his suspicion that he has offended God justified? At that later moment all the poet can say of his hero is:

> breost innan weoll
> þeostrum geþoncum,    swa him geþywe ne wæs.
>
> (2331–2)

[His heart surged internally with dark thoughts, as was not his custom.]

Meanwhile Hrothgar's 'great arrogance grows and spreads' offers no more eventual sustenance than his very similar account of Heremod's fall twenty lines before: 'Yet in his mind his heart's treasure grew fierce and bloody.' The nouns and adjectives are clear enough – 'arrogance' and 'dark' and 'fierce and bloody'. The verbs, however (*weaxeð, wridað, weoll*), remain opaque.

Complaining about this, or straining too hard at the bits of information offered, is as mistaken as trying to wring sense from proverbs through verbal analysis alone. The fact is that though the poet recognizes sensibly that people have an existence outside their social role, his preoccupations are overwhelmingly moral, not psychological, and his morals are based on decisions, results, matters which rise to tangibility. It is therefore characteristic for dilemmas to be dissipated suddenly by action or by gesture. Hrothgar is caught between love and grief at line 1877, and weeps; *he þone breostwylm forberan ne mehte* [he could not restrain the impulse of his heart]. Hengest earlier is caught between rage and promise, and breaks out in murder; *ne meahte wæfre mod forhabban in hreþre* [the restless spirit could not contain itself within his heart]. When he saw his lord in pain, Wiglaf too *ne mihte ða forhabban* [could not then hold back]. As for Beowulf, his 'dark thoughts' end wordlessly in preparing his armour; it is hard to take this as anything but right and proper, like the heroic lack of introspection which the poet tells us is his normal state. In the same way the important fact about Beowulf's thanes in Heorot is that, whatever they thought, they stayed by their leader. Their inner pessimism then only does them credit, just as, a hundred lines later (794–805), their over-optimistic hacking at Grendel is in no sense made foolish by the fact that blades could not harm him. The poet reserves the right to say what people are thinking; he does not, however, regard this as ultimately important.

B

*Money, worth, prestige*

In view of the stress on external factors already noted, it is no surprise to find in the heroes of *Beowulf* a streak of hard materialism. Money hardly appears in the poem; the common Old English word for it, *feoh*, is used by itself three times, but on two of these occasions is immediately qualified by phrases meaning 'ancient treasures', which show that the word carries its vaguer sense of 'valuables'. Yet lack of cash does not preclude a continuing interest in payment from both employers and employed. As soon as Hrothgar hears of Beowulf's arrival he says he will give him treasures for his boldness; his last words before leaving the hero to face Grendel are a promise of lavish reward; he says exactly the same thing to persuade Beowulf to pursue Grendel's mother. Even Wealhtheow feels she has to reinforce her pathetic appeal for help with promises (lines 1220, 1225–6): 'I will remember your reward. . . . I will give you many treasures.' Duty, gratitude, and vengefulness are all present as motives for action, but it is assumed that they have to have tangible support. As for Beowulf, he accepts what he is given, and shows considerable concern about retaining it. When he gets ready to dive into the monsters' lake (1474–91) he thinks first of his men, but second of his property: if he dies, Hrothgar must send it to his next-of-kin.

All natural enough, we might think. However, we should be careful not to let modern reverence for 'economic reality' brainwash us into cynicism. Though Beowulf is careful to collect his winnings, he shows little interest in keeping them. Thus, after Grendel's defeat Hrothgar pays him as bounty a golden banner, a helmet, sword, and mail-shirt, eight horses (one of them saddled), with two gold bracelets and a torque from Wealhtheow. (He also gives something to each of the thanes, and remembers to pay compensation for Hondscio, whom Grendel killed.) The poet still has these objects in mind over a thousand lines later (2152–76), when Beowulf gives nearly all of them away again – four horses and all the military objects to Hygelac, three horses and the torque to Hygd. His sole profit from Grendel appears to be one saddled horse and two bracelets. Admittedly Hygelac gives him a sword in return and 'seven thousand [hides?]', that is, a province to rule, but maybe as one of only two Geatish princes he could have expected that anyway. One might note that Beowulf also misses an easy chance of profit when he returns from Grendel's hall with a head and a sword-hilt and no other treasures at all, 'though he saw many there'. Why are both he and the poet simultaneously so interested in valuables and so stirred by the thought of giving them away? The answer lies in those bugbears of translation, *lof* and *dom*, 'honour', 'glory', 'praise'.

Everyone has noticed the importance of these concepts in the poem. Beowulf himself says that people ought to gain glory before death [*domes ær deaþe*, line 1388]. The poet agrees that 'a man will prosper in every nation through *lofdædum*, praiseworthy deeds' (lines 24–5). To modern ears, trained to consider 'glory-hunting' discreditable, all this sounds ominous, and many have felt that the last word of the poem contains silent reproof, as the Geats say of Beowulf that he was:

> manna mildust     ond monðwærust,
> leodum liðost     ond lofgeornost.          (3181–2)

[The mildest of men and the gentlest, the kindest to his people, and most eager for praise.]

However, the careful and unusual symmetry of the two lines suggests that all four adjectives are meant to be in harmony; the difficulty is no more serious than the nervousness over *druncen* discussed earlier. Acceptance of *lof* and *dom* as absolute goods is nevertheless by no means inconsistent, within the value-scheme of the poem, with a strong interest in 'portable property'.

Consider Beowulf's treatment of the coastguard as he returns from Heorot:

> He þæm batwearde     bunden golde
> swurd gesealde,     þæt he syðþan wæs
> on meodubence     maþme þy weorþra,
> yrfelafe.          (1900–1903)

[He gave that boat-ward a sword bound with gold, so that because of the treasure, the inherited relic, he was from then on *weorþra* on the mead-bench.]

*Weorþra* is the comparative form of the word that descends to modern English as 'worthy'. However, one could hardly say that the man was 'worthier' on the mead-bench; his character is not changed by the present at all. One might say that he was 'worth more', and that would be financially true, but of course not all that is intended. The real point is that the coastguard is more highly esteemed as a result of owning the weapon: it gives him status. And this equation of honour and ownership is entirely characteristic of the poem. When Beowulf receives his first four gifts from Hrothgar, the poet remarks 'he had no need to feel shame before warriors at the treasure he was given' (1025–6), and evidently means that people would respect Beowulf just because of his possessions.

Wulfgar the doorward also assumes that fine feathers make fine birds,
for he tells Hrothgar that his new visitors seem worthy of esteem 'from
their warlike equipment' [on wiggetawum, line 368]. The poet consistently
lets characters make an impression through their weapons, responding
with unfailing admiration to gleaming helmets, bright shields, stacked
spears, linked and shining mail. But his reaction is only partly materialistic:
the objects are offered as an index of honour, inner worth.[2]

All this explains why lof in practice covers 'generosity' as well as
praise; also why the poem has no use for money (which, being neutral,
convertible, and with a value permanently fixed, can tell you nothing
about status); and maybe why Beowulf does not bother to pick up
Grendel's treasure (since it has not been awarded to him, it has about the
same value as a bought Victoria Cross, not negligible, but not complete
either). As for the hero's spendthrift homecoming, obviously if possession
of valuables is a proof of merit, one of the most honourable things you
can do is advertise your resources by giving them away! The poet sees
virtue in lavish donation as well as reception, and thinks it his job to
record both:

> Swa manlice      mære þeoden,
> hordweard hæleþa      heaþoræsas geald
> mearum ond madmum,      swa hy næfre man lyhð,
> se þe secgan wile      soð æfter rihte.                    (1046-9)

[In this noble way the famous lord, treasure-guardian of heroes, paid
for the battle-charges with horses and precious things, as no man will
ever deny – no man who means to tell truth properly.]

A consistent fusion of tangible and intangible is built into the poem's
scenery as into its words. Though the poet never says straight out that
'glory', 'worth', 'treasure', and 'weapons' are all aspects of the same
thing, his phraseology does the job for him: Beowulf is dome gewurpad at
line 1645, just as Hrothgar's saddle is since gewurpad at 1038 and the 'hall-
man' (a tinge of scepticism here) wæpnum gewurpad, 'made to look worthy
by weapons' at 331. Translation must inevitably be cultural as well as
semantic. It is worth noting, though, that this complex of evaluations is
not as alien as it might look. Over the last couple of centuries modern
English has been busily developing the word 'prestige'. This meant
originally 'illusion', but shifted during the nineteenth century in the
direction of 'influence or reputation derived from previous character . . .
or esp. from past successes' (so says the Oxford English Dictionary entry,

[2] This point is made in greater detail by George Clark, 'Beowulf's
Armor', English Literary History 32 (1965), pp. 409-41.

published in 1909). Now, of course, it has become something possessed by men of power and (unlike honour) conferred very largely by the trappings of success – the 'prestigious' car, clothes, wristwatch, home-address. As such it has strong links with *dom* and *lof*. Admittedly, Mr Gladstone in 1878 called 'prestige' a 'base-born thing' and said specifically that it was not to be used in translating ancient epics. However, being 'high-minded' probably spoils more criticism than being 'base-born'. The word is a useful reminder of the way abstracts and objects can mix.

## Swords, halls, and symbols

We are liable to call such mixtures 'symbolism'. Indeed, according to the *OED* a symbol is 'something that stands for, represents, or denotes something else . . . *esp.* a material object representing or taken to represent something immaterial or abstract.' The coastguard's sword is a symbol, then, a material object which everyone takes to represent the abstraction *weorþ*. However, one can easily imagine a member of Beowulfian society insisting that this is not symbolism at all, just matter-of-fact. 'Look' (he might say) 'you wear a sword to show you're ready to fight, and people treat you politely because they can *see* you are. Distinguishing between being ready physically (swords), being ready emotionally (courage), and having social status (honour) – that's just splitting hairs! The three things go together, and if you lose any one of them you'll forfeit the other two very soon.' To return to modern terminology, there is a cause-and-effect relationship between the object and what it represents (like that between wealth and Rolls-Royces). The sword is an 'index' of honour – admittedly a stylized one – rather than a 'symbol' *tout pur*.[3]

This is not just a dispute over vocabulary. We need to keep in mind (as I have said already) that social signs in *Beowulf* function systematically, in systems which cannot be entirely, or even largely, the creation of the poet. The literary associations which 'symbolism' has acquired tend to blur this perception and hinder appreciation. Swords in *Beowulf*, for instance, evidently have a life of their own. The young retainer Wiglaf draws his as he prepares to help his king in the dragon's den; and the poet stops for twenty lines (2611–30) to remark on the weapon's significance. This one was not donated, but first won in battle and then inherited.

[3] These distinctions, and others, are clearly drawn in Jonathan Culler's *Structuralist Poetics* (London 1975), pp. 16–20. Several of the points made in this essay form particular examples of the general procedure Culler recommends.

Accordingly it is a reflection of the courage shown by Wiglaf's father and (given Anglo-Saxon notions of good breeding) a sign of hereditary worth. In the end it becomes totally identified with its owner's personality, so much so, as E. B. Irving has noted,[4] that it does not *weaken* and he does not *melt* – we would have expected these verbs the other way round.

But what happens if you inherit nothing? Since weapons are indexes of honour and status, deprivation of them becomes doubly unendurable. Beowulf himself imagines a scene (2032–69) in which a sword is worn by someone like Wiglaf who had it from his father; but this is seen by the man from whose father's corpse it was gloriously taken. '*Meaht ðu, min wine, mece gecnawan?*' asks a troublemaker [Can you, my friend, recognize that sword?]. He means, 'Are you a man or a mouse?', but neither Beowulf nor the poet bothers to explain this, since everyone knows the next act has to be murder. In exactly the same way the poet feels that the displaying of a sword to Hengest at the climax of the 'Finnsburh Episode' (lines 1143–5) will be self-explanatory. To us, as it happens, it is not; but we can see that the object prompts revenge with irresistible force and in total silence. In *Beowulf* objects can communicate whole chains of abstraction and reflection by their presence alone, and in a way felt by poet and audience to be too natural for words.

Some objects in fact reach 'mythic' status – most obviously, halls. What the poet thinks about these can be derived most immediately from his run of twenty to thirty compound words for describing them. Halls are for drinking in ('winehall', 'beerhall', 'meadhall'); they are filled with people ('guesthall', 'retainer-hall'); in them worth is recognized ('gold-hall', 'gifthall', 'ringhall'). They are also the typical though not the only setting for festivity and for poetry. It is this 'loud merriment in hall' [*dream . . . hludne in healle*] which Grendel hears and hates from the beginning, while Hrothgar's poet sings 'clear in Heorot' on every one of the three nights Beowulf spends there. What he produces is *healgamen* [ the sport (you expect) of halls], and when the Geats look into their gloomy future at the end, the two things they fear to lose are their 'prestigious rings' [*hringweorðung*] and the 'melody of the harp' which, rather implausibly, used to 'wake the warriors' (from their beds on the hall floor, that is, see lines 1237–40). Finally, whether it is from paint or firelight or candles, halls are associated with brightness. Heorot is *goldfah* [gold ornamented], and shines like a beacon: *lixte se leoma ofer landa fela* [the light blazed over many lands]. Inside it is decorated with

4 E. B. Irving Jr, *A Reading of Beowulf* (New Haven and London, 1968), p. 159.

glittering tapestries, *goldfag scinon web after wagum* [on the walls the webs shone golden]. while at line 997 the poet calls it simply *þæt beorhte bold* [the bright building]. In the end the dragon comes to Beowulf's home 'to burn the bright halls' [*beorht hofu bærnan*], and there is a sudden striking image early on of Grendel prowling 'the treasure-ornamented hall on the black nights' [*sincfage sel sweartum nihtum*].

Already one can see how the 'mythic' interpretations come in. The hall equals happiness equals light. What do the monsters which invade halls equal? They are creatures of the night, 'shadow-walkers', 'lurkers in darkness', things which have to be under cover by dawn. It is no great stretch of the imagination to link their darkness with death. Meanwhile the poet's vocabulary, once more, shows an assumption that the happiness of the hall means life. In line 2469 old King Hrethel *gumdream ofgeaf* [gave up the joys of men], his grandson Beowulf (3020–21) 'laid aside laughter, *gamen ond gleodream*, merriment and the joys of song', the Last Survivor's kinsmen (2252) 'gave up this life, *gesawon seledream*, had seen the joy of the hall'. The compound words show how tightly men and harps and halls cluster together in the poet's mind, and presumably in his audience's. A similar familiarity informs the untranslated and possibly unconscious metaphor near the end, when the poet ruminates that it is a mystery where we all must go:

> þonne leng ne mæg
> mon mid his magum     meduseld buan.          (3064–5)

[When a man can no longer, with his kinsmen, inhabit the meadhall.]

*Meduseld* is semantically indistinguishable from its familiar precursors *medoærn*, *medoheal*. By this time, however, what it means is 'Life-Gone-By'. The poet has no need to explain.

Halls are 'indexes' of happiness, then, because in them people are most likely to be free from poverty. They are 'symbols' too, because they are crowded with not entirely realistic conventional signs, like harps and gold and brightness. Their vulnerability implies a shared social myth about the limits of human capacity (stated most overtly by the councillor of King Edwin in Bede).[5] However, they remain at all times stubborn and solid facts, things which could be seen in reality as well as heard about in poetry. It is important that literal-minded Anglo-Saxons could always take halls literally, because what they would get from *Beowulf* was not the

---

[5] Bede, *A History of the English Church and People* (Penguin Classics translated by L. Sherley-Price, revised edn Harmondsworth, 1968), Book 2, Chapter 13. See further Kathryn Hume, 'The Concept of the Hall in Old English Poetry', *Anglo-Saxon England* 3 (1974), pp. 63–74.

notion that Heorot was like life, but the more searching one that life was
like Heorot. 'We too', they might conclude, 'live in a little circle of light.
Every time we go to sleep expecting to wake up, we could be as wrong
as Hrothgar's retainers. Æschere is us.' Involvement of this nature
deepens many of the scenes in the poem. Modern readers no longer reach
it naturally and wordlessly, but they are not completely immune to it
either. Professor Tolkien's 'Golden Hall' in the second volume of *The
Lord of the Rings* is still called 'Meduseld', and the name still has its
power.

## Allusion and reality

The ethics, behaviour, and vocabulary of Beowulfian characters all hang
together, create strong *vraisemblance*. Of course the poet also delights in
deliberate fantasy, in things which never happened and never could –
the blade melting in Grendel's corrosive blood, the robber stepping
cautiously past the sleeping dragon's head, the monsters' dream of
banquet on the sea-bottom. Most famous perhaps is Hrothgar's evocation
of that classic motif of horror-story, the animal whose instincts perceive
something that human senses cannot. Though the hunted hart may come
to the edge of the ominous mere, he says:

>               'ær he feorh seleð,
> aldor on ofre,     ær he in wille,
> hafelan beorgan;     nis þæt heoru stow!'    (1370–72)

[Rather will he give up his life and spirit on the shore than plunge in
to save his head; it is an uncanny spot!]

And yet even this fantasia is obeying a fundamental principle of realistic
fiction: it implies a depth of memory for Hrothgar to draw on, creatures
and landscapes which exist outside the poem's needs, and consequently a
weight of fact which urges the reader to think 'this must be true'. One
wonders how much of the poem's impression of realism is as artificially
created.

Consider the poem's most redundant character, Yrmenlaf. He appears
only in line 1324, as Hrothgar reacts rather crossly to Beowulf's un-
fortunate 'Have you had a pleasant night?' 'Don't ask about pleasure', he
says. 'Sorrow is renewed for the Danish people. Dead is Æschere,
Yrmenlaf's elder brother, my confidant, my counsellor, who stood at my
shoulder. . . .' In the poem Æschere himself functions only as corpse, and
it shows a certain conscientiousness on the part of the poet to award him
six and a half lines of elegy, as he does. But why bring in his *younger
brother*? Is this realism again – the outright invention of corroborating

detail? Or is it a sudden appeal to a frame of knowledge existing outside the poem, in which Yrmenlaf was a sort of Pellinore or Bedivere of Danish legend – not a prominent person, but one known to exist?

Obviously no one can say, and it hardly matters, since in that context invention and reminder would work just about as well. However, our uncertainty over Yrmenlaf's very existence dramatizes a series of linked and vital questions of a much more general kind. Is the world of *Beowulf* a never-never land created by the poet? Did the original audience know a version of history into which *Beowulf* had to fit? Most important of all, did the poet *and* his original audience feel that the characters in the poem were in essence men like themselves, or did they see them as irrevocably different, fictional creatures of an imaginary society? Answers to these questions cannot be simple.

There are three immediate reasons, though, for taking a broadly 'fictive' and 'distanced' view. Nearly all critics agree that the poet must have been a literate Christian Englishman. But if you judged from internal evidence alone you might conclude that he had never been to Britain; had never heard of Christ; and was not exactly sure what 'writing' meant. These statements need some qualification. There *is* an Englishman in the poem, that Offa (he gets a mention in lines 1944–62) who according to *Widsith* 'ruled the English' [*weold Ongle*]. However, *Widsith* also makes clear that Offa lived near the Eider in Schleswig-Holstein; he 'ruled the English' before they migrated to England. Similarly, though the poem contains no books, it does use the verb *writan*. But this seems to mean 'cut' not 'write'. Beowulf 'forwrote' the worm (line 2705), that is, he cut it in two. When the poet says of the giant sword-hilt 'on it was *writen* the origin of that far-off fight', he may mean it had a picture 'engraved' on it. The *runstafas* of line 1695 (are they 'secret staves' or 'runic letters'?) only spell out the maker's name. As for *scrifan* (modern German *schreiben*), it means 'judge, sentence, condemn'. The absence of references to Christ is even more puzzling, for it co-exists with repeated references to God, the devil, the Flood, Cain and Abel. There can be no doubt that the poet *did* know about Christ, and England, and book-learning; his omission of all three indicates a consciousness of anachronism between his own time and that of his story.

Yet in other respects the poet and the characters are very closely identified. It may not seem so at first, for right at the beginning we can feel the narrator seizing control. *He* is the man who knows what is happening across the sea, in the future, in the darkness or within men's hearts. Connecting causes and effects comes naturally to him (see line 7), while he does not find even God's purposes inscrutable (see lines 13–17).

The narrator, in brief, knows nearly everything and nearly everybody. When he uses the adjective *nathwylc*, literally 'I-know-not-which', it is evident that he also means 'and the information is of no importance'; 'some slave or other' stole the dragon's gold and 'some man or other' hid it in the first place. And yet this near-omniscience comes over as only a developed form of a quality which many men are expected to share, and to which the narrator thinks he can make occasional appeal. Wulfgar appears momentarily, and the narrator observes that his courage and wisdom were 'known to many' [*manegum gecyðed*]; Beowulf says his father was called Ecgtheow, and 'many a wise man on earth still remembers him'. They may both be wrong, of course, but they are inviting corroboration or contradiction from somewhere. Hrothgar's ecyclopaedic knowledge, meanwhile, rivals the narrator's; *he* remembers Ecgtheow, shows traces of prophetic ability, confidently detects the intentions of God. His courtiers show exactly the same comparative tendencies as the poet, for just as the latter says again and again that he has never heard of a greater treasure or a more lavish ship-burial or friendlier donations, so the racing thanes say there is no better man than Beowulf, and enshrine their opinion in impromptu verse. It would, indeed, be merely dull not to recognize that the *cyninges pegn* of line 867 is a 'disguised narrator'.[6] What he says is what the poet wants us to know, and several of the imagined speakers in *Beowulf* have exactly the same direct but undramatic role – most obviously Hrothgar in lines 1700-84, the Last Survivor (2247-66), the anonymous Messenger (2900-3027). It is no wonder that no one in the poem responds to any of those speeches, nor that the poet on occasion ticks them overtly as correct – *he ne leag fela wyrda ne worda* [he was not far wrong in words or of events], or in other words 'that bit can be relied on'.

The narrator and his characters create what amounts to a continuum – the poem of *Beowulf* at one end, at the other nameless gossip like that about Offa's taming of his queen:

> ealodrincende          oðer sædan,
> þæt hio leodbealewa          læs gefremede. . . .          (1945-6)

[The beer-drinkers told a different tale, that she performed fewer outrages on her people.]

Between the two lies an entire and well imagined complex of legendary tradition arising out of contemporary judgement. Of course this could all be a trick – a device of the Flaubertian 'poet' who is silently surveying

[6] This concept is explained by Wayne C. Booth, *The Rhetoric of Fiction* (Chicago, 1961), p. 152.

the universe of 'narrator' and 'characters' without ever appearing in it. But it seems more plausible to think the image is in essence true. The poet after all repeatedly equates truth and poetry through the words *sop* and *riht* (see lines 871, 1049, 2107-10), and begins by including his audience with himself in the *we* of *Beowulf*'s first two lines: 'Listen, we have heard of the might of the kings of the Spear-Danes in ancient days. . . .' Again no one can say for sure that these informed listeners are not imaginary too! But they fit in well with the poet's projected image of himself and his characters. Behind them all lies an expanse of legendary tradition, not an abstract force but one repeatedly incarnated in figures like the *ealodrincende*, or the 'old land-guardian' of line 1702, who 'remembers everything' and 'advances truth and right among the people' – a culture-bearer, a poet in embryo, a link between real present and just-as-real past.

All this is not to decry the author's originality, nor the very great scope he allows to fiction and to fantasy. Like the hunted hart, the Danish coastguard and Æschere's brother and quite possibly Beowulf himself are born from his imagination into the clear but bounded light of legendary poetry. Nevertheless, it looks as if neither the poet nor his audience would tolerate anything that contradicted too sharply history as they already knew it, while though the world of the poem is no doubt stylized, its social and physical furniture are not merely personal inventions. Most important, we can reasonably suspect that the poet and his audience felt 'continuity', if not identity, with dead heroes. They knew all these things happened 'long ago' [*on geardagum*], and that 'in those days' [*þy dogore*, line 1797] some things were different. On the other hand, even in history an eternal stability ruled men and seasons 'as it does still' [*swa he nu gen deð*, lines 1058, 1134, 2859].[7] Furthermore, when the poet says approvingly of Wulfgar 'he knew court custom' [*cuþe he duguðe þeaw*, 359], clearly he does not mean that *particular* court's custom, he means everybody's. Learning and geography change, we might conclude, but in *Beowulf* etiquette at least is felt to remain fixed and standard.

[7] For a more detailed treatment of these variations in authorial distance, see Stanley B. Greenfield, 'The authenticating voice in *Beowulf*', *Anglo-Saxon England* 5 (1976), pp. 51-62.

# 3. The Structure of the Poem

*Balance and interlace*

Viewing the solidity and consistency of the Beowulfian world is a useful preparative for considering the Beowulfian plot, which at first sight and even at second exhibits neither of those qualities. It is almost indecently paraphrasable as 'three fights with three monsters', and yet no matter how much you compress it, it still looks broken-backed; there is no relationship between the second and the third fight at all, while there is a gap in the middle that far outdoes Shakespeare's *Winter's Tale* – 'fifty winters' skimmed over in ten lines. As Aristotle put it, 'the unity of a plot does not consist, as some suppose, in its having one man as its subject'. It is therefore no wonder that critics of *Beowulf* have been quick to look for some supra-chronological unity informing the poem.

Professor Tolkien suggested that the guiding principle was 'balance' or 'opposition' – 'a contrasted description of two moments in a great life, rising and setting; an elaboration of the ancient and intensely moving contrast between youth and age, first achievement and final death.'[1] This theory has the advantage of concentrating on the poem's essential concerns (the hero and the monsters), but makes the poem seem 'static', if 'diversified', or as Tolkien said (speaking of Old English metre as a whole) 'more like masonry than music'. Yet most readers of *Beowulf* take from it an impression of intricacy; accordingly a more popular artistic analogue has been that suggested by John Leyerle in 1967, interweaving or 'interlace'.[2]

This last word refers to a mode practised by innumerable English masons and illustrators during the seventh and eighth centuries, reaching a peak in such manuscripts as the Lindisfarne Gospels, and having as its main characteristics the absence of any visual centre, luxuriant and coiling repetitions, an elusive patterning which defies attempts to perceive the whole design at once. The main reason for linking this mode with

[1] J. R. R. Tolkien, '*Beowulf*: the Monsters and the Critics', *Proceedings of the British Academy* 22 (1936), pp. 245–95.
[2] See J. Leyerle, 'The Interlace Structure of *Beowulf*', *University of Toronto Quarterly* 37 (1967), pp. 1–17.

*Beowulf* is that though the central plot of that poem is simple, our response to it is qualified or even prevented by an enormous web of memory, prophecy, and incidental reference from the poet-narrator (the power of whose authorial control has been noted). It is this which makes reading *Beowulf* a distinctive literary experience, and accordingly (though at times it looks as if they are agreeing with W. P. Ker, that the poet put 'the irrelevancies in the centre and the serious things on the outer edges') nearly all modern critics base their readings of the poem on its peripheries, its allusions, the side-references we are no longer allowed to call 'digressions'.

## The implications of digression

An entirely typical example of these occurs within the first hundred lines. Hrothgar, king of the Danes, has decided to build his great hall of Heorot, has given the orders, seen them carried out, and taken possession – 'the hall towered, high, horn-gabled'. Then without syntactic warning or detectable change of tone the poet abandons Hrothgar's triumphant progress to remark:

> heaðowylma bad,
> laðan liges;  ne wæs hit lenge þa gen,
> þæt se ecghete  aþumsweoran
> æfter wælniðe  wæcnan scolde. (82–5)

[It waited for the battle-waves, the hateful fire. It was not for a long time yet that the armed hatred of son-in-law and father-in-law should awaken after deadly spite.]

Much could be said about these few words. They contain a certain reassurance: it was not for a long time yet that trouble would come. But the verbs are menacing. The hall is like a sentient creature that knows its fate, for it is 'waiting' for the fire all the time, while hatred also has life, for it will 'wake' after sleep. The reassurance and the menace together create a sense of time as *long*, stretching out indefinitely into Heorot's future, but also as *single*, comprehended by the poet's vision and containing within it events, like buildings and burnings, which only appear unrelated. The passage's disturbing effect is made greater by its context: the next line, 86, introduces Grendel lurking outside Heorot in the darkness.

However, even these reactions are likely to be overshadowed, for us, by the realization that we do not know what the poet is talking about. We have to start 'reconstructing' from the word *aþumsweoran*, a word

never used elsewhere in Anglo-Saxon, and not really used in our copy of
*Beowulf* either, since the scribe misunderstood it and wrote instead the
common but here meaningless phrase *aþum swerian* [to swear by oaths].
Still, *aþum-sweoran* would be a word of familiar type, a 'dvandva'
compound connecting two words for family relationship, *aþum* [son-in-
law] and *sweor* [father-in-law]. Who are these two people? One of them
ought to be the owner of the hall; the only known owner is the first one,
Hrothgar; he is too old to be a likely son-in-law; so perhaps (it can be
seen what a feeble chain of reasoning this is) he is the *sweor* half of the
compound. Nearly two thousand lines later Beowulf remarks that
Hrothgar indeed has a daughter, Freawaru, promised but not yet
married to the 'fortunate son of Froda'. Irritatingly, Beowulf still does
not give this man's name; but forty lines on he lets slip that the prospective
son-in-law is called Ingeld.

Here we come on to firmer ground, for Ingeld is a well known figure
of Northern heroic legend; *Widsith* says explicitly that he was defeated by
Hrothgar at Heorot. It does not say that Heorot was burnt down, or that
Ingeld and Hrothgar were related, but the cross-reference gives a little
strength to our chain of reconstructions. The real point here, though, is
that the whole process just outlined is artificial; a conclusion we must
draw is that the poet did not expect his audience to react like that at all, but
assumed its members knew of Heorot and Hrothgar and Ingeld already.
He had only to mention the first two and hint at the third for a story to
rise from their memories.

Outside knowledge at that point only makes the little allusion more
frightening. Upon the image of size and splendour and novelty which
the poet has made one is being asked to superimpose an opposite one of
pain and fire and finality. The fact that (if you are familiar with heroic
legend) this last image comes from outside the poem, indeed from your
own brain, and that you are being asked to recognize the two as still, in a
sense, 'the same' – this creates for modern reader or Anglo-Saxon one a
shocking if momentary sense of callous reality enclosing Heorot, wider
even than the poem itself. Then the insight vanishes as we are returned
to the main story. But can that main story ever seem the same again?
The poet says no more about the fate of Heorot, indeed he re-establishes
its brilliance and comfort lovingly and at length. Still, no one can say
the fire is not as real as the festivity; it could be reintroduced at any
time.

Such temporal switchings become increasingly important as the poem
goes on. One almost identical with that quoted is the passage 1202–14,
which centres on the gold torque given to Beowulf for killing Grendel.

This particular *maððum* is the climax of the first string of donations, stressed by the poet's admiring comment that he has never heard of a greater treasure since ... – and he mentions a necklace famous in mythology. But just as with Heorot, as soon as the image of beauty is established the poet superimposes on it death and disaster:

> Þone hring hæfde      Higelac Geata,
> nefa Swertinges      nyhstan siðe,
> siðþan he under segne      sinc ealgode,
> wælreaf werede;      hyne wyrd fornam ...      (1202–5)

[Hygelac of the Geats had that ring, Swerting's grandson, on his last journey, when he defended treasure under his banner, fought for his booty; fate took him.]

The poet goes on to tell the story of a fatal raid on Frisia, in which Hygelac was killed, the Geats defeated, and the necklace now given to Beowulf stripped from his uncle's body by the victorious Franks.

*This* 'digression' owes its fame among modern critics to the coincidental fact that for once we can say, not 'there must have been a story about it', but 'this is true, it really happened'. Against all odds of probability Hygelac turns up in recognizable form as the pirate 'Chlochilaicus' whose raid on the Frisians and defeat by the Franks is recorded in Latin chronicle by Gregory of Tours, an event of around AD 526.[3] However, the literary questions it arouses are, first, how much we should let this insight into disaster colour our perception of Beowulf's later honours and triumphs, and second, whether we might not in a way have been prepared for it already.

To explain this latter: I have remarked already that Hygelac is Beowulf's uncle, indeed his mother's brother (a relation of special intimacy to Anglo-Saxons). But that fact is not deducible from internal evidence alone at line 1202. We know who Beowulf is, for Hrothgar has explained his descent with suspicious care. We also know that Hygelac is king of the Geats, and that Beowulf is devoted to him, tends indeed to define himself by referring to him (see lines 261, 343, 407). But we have never been told that Hygelac is 'the son of Hrethel', the vital piece of information expressed rather casually at line 1485. It looks as if, like Ingeld, Hygelac was meant to be familiar already. If that was so, his death would be a known fact too. And if *that* was so (this is 'reconstruction' again), every time Beowulf in the early lines of the poem expresses emotional dependence on his king, he is betraying a vulnerability at odds

---

[3] See R. W. Chambers, *Beowulf: an Introduction* (3rd edn with supplement by C. L. Wrenn, Cambridge, 1959), pp. 2–4.

with his evident strength and confidence. He has an Achilles' heel, in short, though he does not know it.

That speculation contains too many unknowns to be relied on. What is clear, though, is that the poet exploits the gap between his audience's awareness of the Frisian fiasco and Beowulf's unawareness of it in at least one later scene, when Beowulf, having fought his second fight against Grendel's mother, is about to leave Denmark. His farewell to Hrothgar (lines 1818–39) can be paraphrased as follows: (1) 'thank you for your hospitality' (2) 'if I can do anything else for you, I will' (3) 'if I hear you are attacked, I will bring an army to your assistance – Hygelac will ratify this' (4) 'we Geats would be pleased to entertain your son in our country'. The key-word in all this is *wat*. Beowulf says: 'I know [*ic wat*] of Hygelac, lord of the Geats, keeper of the people, young though he may be, that he will support me in this, so that I can do you honour, bring a wood of spears to your assistance. . . .' The audience, though, knows something different – that soon Hygelac will be past helping anyone. So does Hrothgar, the old king, the wise king. He praises and thanks Beowulf for his offer, but there is temperance in his enthusiasm. He remarks, indeed, that if the spear *should* remove Hygelac, and Beowulf *should* survive, then the Geats could not have a better substitute – assuming that Beowulf was prepared to succeed. This is too accurate for the poet not to want us to notice; all Hrothgar's hypotheses, down to Beowulf's survival and his reluctance to take the throne, come true. The whole scene therefore works on two levels, with justified optimism from both speakers in the foreground, but behind it an awareness in the audience that Hrothgar is closer to the truths of history than Beowulf. This could not happen without the necklace passage six hundred lines before; but once Hygelac *is* connected with failure mention of him can never be neutral or carefree again.

One can then go further and say that the leave-taking scene actually works on *three* levels. But this assertion depends on another character (the blankest in the poem as Yrmenlaf is the most redundant) – Hrothulf. The poet never explains who he is. At line 1017 he is drinking many a cup with Hrothgar in the high hall, which (given the evident ritualism of drink ceremonies in *Beowulf*) may indicate a degree of power-sharing. At lines 1163–4 he and Hrothgar must be the *suhtergefæderan* – another 'dvandva' compound meaning 'uncle and nephew' – which makes him the son of one of Hrothgar's (dead) brothers, Heorogar or Halga. Since King Hrólfr Helgason, nephew of King Hróarr, is a famous figure of legend, all scholars assume the latter. But this admission of Scandinavian legends prompts blacker thoughts, for in them the sons of Hrothgar/

Hróarr never appear at all, the kingship going direct from uncle to
nephew. This could be legal in Old Danish society, but it could also have
been accompanied by murder. It is not hard to imagine a legend in which
all the Scyldings wiped each other out; and though some scholars find
such 'reconstructions' illegitimate, they are (as we have seen) in *Beowulf*
both common and compelled. Ominousness is in any case deliberately
stimulated by the third and last reference to Hrothulf, inside Wealhtheow's speech of 1169–87. Once one has made allowance for the
conventions of politeness which govern this, no one can mistake its tone
of fear.[4] The Danish queen is even afraid of Beowulf because Hrothgar
has offered to adopt him 'as a son' [*for sunu*], a phrase she pointedly
repeats; and her anxiety about her sons' future is stimulated further by
Hrothulf, whom she asks to protect them – though he does not reply.
Without any analogues at all one would see this speech as uneasy, and
with them it becomes at once alarming and pathetic.

   Is that why Beowulf, taking his leave six hundred lines later, suggests
that Hrothgar's son Hrethric would do well to leave home? If it is, it
makes the dialogue between young hero and old king even more
pointed, as Hrothgar sees the danger hanging over Beowulf (that
Hygelac is going to die), and Beowulf reciprocally sees the danger over
Hrothgar (that he cannot ensure the succession of his sons). *But neither
sees the point of the other's warning!* If that *is* the case, one of the least-
stressed scenes in the poem turns out to be almost unbearably loaded with
hidden meanings; though these, it should be noted, are exactly parallel
with the poet's brief and open remark about Heorot at the start.

   One can see now why 'interlace' is such an attractive image for the
structure of *Beowulf*. Time and again a passage from one part of the poem
reverberates in and alters another. But the threads of connection are
discontinuous, for while the monsters are 'on-stage' we forget about
Heorot and Hrothulf and all the rest. They are unpredictable too, for you
never know when the poet will bring on a new character (like Ingeld),
or an insight to change retrospectively your perception of what has gone
before (like Beowulf's reliance on Hygelac). Finally, there is a sense in
which the pattern of the poem can only be completed outside it, in the
stories to which the poet appeals and in the experience of history which
encloses characters and poem at once.

   There are then two caveats to enter. One is that many more 'inter-
lacings' can be discovered between passages which have not been
discussed and even between those which have. Wealhtheow relates

4 For analysis see Irving, *A Reading of Beowulf*, op. cit., pp. 136–41, and
further T. A. Shippey, *Old English Verse* (London, 1972), pp. 33–4.

thematically with her daughter Freawaru, for instance, through their shared vulnerability, and is juxtaposed with a third 'unhappy lady', Hildeburh, not-quite-heroine of a story sung in Heorot (lines 1068–1159). The kernel of *that* story, furthermore, is one of the sword-presentation scenes already mentioned, which run with evident comparability through the entire poem. At times one feels the 'interlaces' of *Beowulf* increase geometrically.

The second caveat, though, is that in the hands of modern literary critics this admitted feature of the poem's structure is often drawn out with grotesque laboriousness, every incident being dwelt on till it renders up all individual life to a generalized background of 'significance'. All the passages mentioned here contain one of two things – an object which unites contrasted moments (Heorot or the torque), or a speech with both overt and covert purpose (thanks/warning, congratulation/appeal). In either case something remains 'the same' beneath conflicting interpretations, to focus attention and assist the memory. Dark Age audiences have had great strain placed on their knowledge and sensitivity in all that has been said about the complicated histories of one royal house and another. Of course in those times people had to be cleverer to survive. Still, they also had to respond without study-aids. Subtlety in the pursuit of abstractions (especially dully moral ones) should not be pressed too far.

## The ironic image

That is why the whole of the foregoing discussion has been conducted without the term 'irony', so often the bane of Beowulfians. It means too many things to too many people, and though some of its meanings are appropriate and even vital to reading the poem, others which shelter under the same semantic umbrella turn out misleading, or worse.[5]

Thus, the element of 'innocence' or 'confident unawareness' which pre-eminently distinguishes victims of irony is all but endemic at least in the first two thousand lines. Beowulf relying on Hygelac, the Danes lying down in Heorot, Hrothgar carefully planning the peace-initiatives to Ingeld – all these offer classic instances of ironic discrepancy between the perception of characters and the knowledge of observers. In the same way juxtaposition of 'appearance and reality' is strong in the poem from the first mention of Heorot's burning; everything *looks* solid enough, but we know it is only temporary. Finally, ironic comedy is deliberately

---

[5] The discussion that follows relies on D. C. Muecke's two books, *The Compass of Irony* (London, 1969), and *Irony* (Critical Idiom Series 13, London, 1970).

entertained by the poet in the account of Grendel's approach to Heorot. He 'meant' to catch a man, we are told, 'it was not the first time' he had done so, he 'laughed' in his heart on seeing the sleeping Geats, for 'feast-full expectation' came upon him. All the time 'the mighty kinsman of Hygelac' lies waiting, and we know that Grendel's hopes must fail. On this evidence there is good reason for granting the poet the status of a conscious and practised literary ironist.

On the other hand he does seem to avoid one device which is vital to ironists of later date: he never presents as right things known to be wrong. 'It is a truth universally acknowledged,' declares Jane Austen, 'that a single man in possession of a good fortune, must be in want of a wife.' This is not 'universally acknowledged' at all: to spell the point out, only mothers of economically dependent daughters are likely to think that way, and irony comes from the reader's perception of the gap between their wishes and reality, or between their pretended concern for bachelors and their underlying self-interest. But when the *Beowulf*-poet says 'in every nation a man will get on through generous deeds', though his *mægþa gehwære* is very like Jane Austen's 'universally acknowledged', there is every sign that he means it straight. His art, as has been said, consistently lays claim to truth.

Yet it is not *impossible* to read his plain statements ironically. That, indeed, is why 'irony' is a dangerous term. Just like proverbs, ironies depend on an extra-linguistic frame: we perceive as ironic what we are reluctant to perceive as true, and perception of truth is, notoriously, relative. Accordingly even the Beowulfian statement just quoted *could* be read ironically; at that stage of the poem (one might say) heroism is still untarnished, the purchase of warriors by gifts still seems excellent advice. The body of the poem, however, will prove that 'the wages of heroism is death' and that kings' generosity is bought too dear. So when the poet ends by calling Beowulf 'most eager for praise', he must mean us to see that that eagerness has been his bane. The *lofgeornost* of the end and the *lofdædum* of the start create an 'ironic perspective'; the poet's initial 'gnome' must be as false as Jane Austen's! So one might argue, and there would be no disproving it. All *that* proves, however, is that irony is socially determined. *Þæt wæs god cyning* could mean 'he was a bad king', just as 'you're a fine friend' now usually means 'you let me down'. This inability to judge plain statements brings us, in fact, upon the great divide of *Beowulf* criticism. Is the poem epic or satire, celebration or critique? In view of what has just been said, it ought to be clear that 'close reading' alone will not lead to a decision.

A common train of thought, however, starts from the word 'heathen' [*hæþen*]. This implies inevitably a sense of distance and moral superiority; only Christians use it and only of non-Christians. The poet uses it of Hrothgar's Danes. Under the strain of Grendel's murders, he says, they asked the devil to help them, for 'such was their custom, the hope of the heathens [*hæþenra hyht*]'. There is no doubt, therefore, that he feels superior to them, and views their behaviour with conscious irony as deluded, idolatrous, counter-productive. Does he think like that about Beowulf and Hrothgar and Hygelac as well? He should: for their historical counterparts must have *been* heathen, the absence of references to Christ indicates he knew as much, and (in the famous words of Alcuin, speaking as it happens of Ingeld) *non vult rex celestis cum paganis et perditis nominetenus regibus communionem habere* [the King of Heaven will have no fellowship at all with damned and heathen kings]. The poet admittedly never says directly that he is a sheep and his characters are goats; but anyone who calls other people 'heathens' is bound to view 'heathenness' as somehow reprehensible, even if he also repeatedly calls his heroes 'good'.

An idea which fits the circumstances (and one familiar in our century) is that of social guilt. Beowulf and his friends, in other words, are excellent individually, but so involved in the violence of a vengeful and Christ-less society that they cannot break out of it. The admiration so often expressed in the poem for halls and weapons and courtesies must then be theirs; but it should strike the outside observers of the audience as increasingly superficial the more they see the halls burning, the courtesies failing, the weapons being used. Is it not, after all, a fact that the royal houses of Denmark, Sweden, Geatland, wipe each other out? The heroes' behaviour is compulsive and (once more ironically) it is Beowulf himself who articulates the compulsion with his briskly proverbial speech of lines 1384–96:

> 'Selre bið æghwæm,
> þæt he his freond wrece,      þonne he fela murne.'      (1384–5)

[Better for anyone to avenge his friend than mourn too much.]

Fifty years later, of course, this same belief will lead Swedes and Franks to overthrow Beowulf's own people. But, though he is quick enough to deplore Ingeld's commitment to revenge in lines 2029–31, Beowulf is too much a part of 'the heroic system' to be aware of its and his own contradictions. We have to be aware of them for him.

So the theory goes, and it draws further reinforcement from Beowulf's uncle Hygelac, whose job (in this view) is to show how unnatural peace in the heroic world has become. Why did he raid Frisia and get himself killed? As far as we can see, it was not thirst for vengeance, but plain piracy. *He for wlenco wean ahsode*, says the poet, 'he looked for trouble out of pride'. But what caused his pride and his piracy if not that he needed money to pay his men? The centre of society is after all the hall, and the hall's function is to be a centre for gift-giving. But the king's exemplary lavishness needs constant restocking, and since the gifts his men expect are above all weapons and armour, the natural concomitant of generosity is robbery-with-violence. King and retainers, then, are unwitting accomplices in a cycle which moves from hall to battlefield and which continually supplies initial impetus to feuds which then develop their own. A grim picture, but a plausible one; it also contains a final irony aimed at Beowulf himself.

For he at least does not promote his kingship by piracy, and though he takes revenge twice after coming to the throne (once on the Swedes, once on the dragon), both times he is finishing a feud he did not start. Yet he too dies betrayed. Why this injustice? The unpalatable answer suggested once again is 'pride', for though Beowulf is ready to think the dragon may be divine punishment (lines 2329–32), he still will not – so Wiglaf says later (3079–83) – simply leave it alone. Very proper too, perhaps, except that Beowulf is not the only one to suffer from his own excessive zeal; he leaves his country wide open to tragedy. As Wiglaf sums up:

> 'Oft sceall eorl monig       anes willan
> wræc adreogan,       swa us geworden is.'       (3077–8)

[Often many a man has to suffer misery from the desire of one, as has happened to us.]

He means, maybe, that though there is no excuse for the retainers who let Beowulf down, still he in turn let *them* down, even if his vice once more sprang from good intentions. Just as Hygelac's piracy is the other half of kingly generosity, so the obverse of Beowulf's admirable fearlessness is narrowness of vision, concern for the bubble reputation. Heroes, in short, make bad kings. Unfortunately kings are expected to be heroes; and if they shirk that obligation, outsiders will probably force it on them.[6]

Such wry morals as these are drawn easily from comparative consideration of Beowulf, Hrothgar, Hygelac. The whole 'interlace' structure encourages them. They make us think that the poet is demonstrating the inadequacy of heroic society; that he sees this the more

[6] For a thorough presentation of this opinion, see John Leyerle's 'Beowulf the Hero and the King', *Medium Aevum* 34 (1965), pp. 89–102.

forcibly for being a Christian; and that his rejection of overt finger-pointing first gives you the pleasure of ironic perception, and second shows you the glittering insidiousness of heroism, the way it perverts even the best of intentions. This whole approach offers evidently attractive baits, propounding an interesting sociological thesis, rejecting the cult of violence, and making it possible to give the poet immense credit for conscious artistry. It is, however, dependent at every stage on silent and unproven ironies. One may reflect sceptically that it all seems very up-to-date.

### Performatives and perceptions

In practice there are strong arguments against all the propositions just advanced. *Wlenco*, the emotion which prompts Hygelac's fatal raid, may not be a vice at all (Wulfgar does not think so at line 338); the Geatish dismay at Beowulf's death could be just a flattering reflection of his indispensability; the poet may be as blind to the abstract implications of his story as are his characters. But, as has been said, there is no sure way of proving when irony is intended and when it is not. More constructively, we should note the presence in *Beowulf* of different styles of emotion and changing narrative modes.

Consider, for instance, the end (already quoted) of Wealhtheow's speech, lines 1216–31. She has just spoken to Hrothgar about the danger of introducing rivals to her sons. She has also given Beowulf the great torque, for the poet to comment on its unlucky future. Then she speaks again, moving from praise of Beowulf to appeal for his help:

> 'Beo þu suna minum
> dædum gedefe,     dreamhealdende!
> Her is æghwylc eorl     oþrum getrywe,
> modes milde,     mandrihtne hold,
> þegnas syndon geþwære,     þeod ealgearo,
> druncne dryhtguman     doð swa ic bidde.' (1226–31)

[Be kind to my son in your deeds, guard him in joy! Here every warrior is true to the next, kind in heart and loyal to his lord, the thanes are united, the people all willing, the drunken retainers do as I say.]

This is ironic, in a sense. Certainly we need not believe it, for 'here' is Heorot, and among those present are Hrothulf and the sinister Unferth, about whose loyalty almost everyone has doubts. Still, it is hard to cast Wealhtheow as a *victim* of irony in the same way as Beowulf in that scene is; for while he remains innocently confident in Hygelac's immortality, her preoccupation with her sons radiates awareness of danger. Why then does she come out with these last four lines of peace and security? The speech could have ended with fine pathos at *dreamhealdende*.

The answer, surely, is that in them she is striving to evoke the *dream* for which she so desperately wishes. All spells proceed from the belief that if you say something the right way, it will come true, and that is what she is doing. For a moment, too, it works. Wealhtheow's pause eternizes that 'best of feasts' like Keats's Grecian Urn. The poet ratifies her perception fifteen lines later, as the Danish thanes 'pile arms' before going to sleep: 'It was their custom to be often ready for war, whether at home or on campaign, either one, just as often as need dictated to their lord: that was a noble nation.' Of course an ironist could take even *wæs seo þeod tilu* as critical (for those who live by the sword shall die by it). In context, though, it is regretful. A proper conclusion would be that, just as the lines on Heorot's burning made future fire as real as present festivity, so these make past festivity as real as present non-existence. Positives have value too; and transience does not make happiness the same as grief.

That short section makes an impact even in the doom-laden 'trough' of Heorot between Grendel and Grendel's mother. It ought to be noted that a similar but much stronger impact is made by the next 'trough', the account of Beowulf's homecoming in lines 1888–2199. Even Tolkien could not find for this any 'complete justification', while Kenneth Sisam said it was 'unsuccessful' and 'lifeless'.[7] Yet in spite of its narrative sluggishness, the section works emotionally as the poem's 'warm centre' – a place from which irony is excluded. It introduces to us Hygelac's queen Hygd, as young and wise as her husband is young and valiant; continues with an idyllic picture of Hygelac and Beowulf sitting as kinsmen together, *mæg wið mæge*, while the queen offers drink lovingly to the retainers in turn; and goes on through Beowulf's adventures to his open profession of devotion: 'Still all my happiness depends on you; I have few close kinsmen, Hygelac, but you.' The repeated *ðe/ðec* of lines 2149–51 is by modern standards almost dog-like. Beowulf backs it up, though, by giving Hygelac most of what he has won. And quite right too, bursts in the poet irrepressibly (2166–8). 'So *shall* a kinsman do – not prepare webs of treachery for others with secret craft!' That, we might think, is the way the Scyldings behave. But Hygelac's hall is opposite to Heorot point for point. In it nephew is loyal to uncle (2170), and vice-versa (2171); its queen has no need to ask for help; the unity it

7 Tolkien, *op. cit.*, p. 272; K. Sisam, *The Structure of Beowulf* (Oxford, 1965), pp. 44–5.

represents lets even cousins (Beowulf and Heardred) stay friends. Indeed
the best proof of Geatish unity comes from the royal carelessness of
demarcation:

> Him wæs bam samod
> on ðam leodscipe     lond gecynde,
> eard eðelriht,     oðrum swiðor
> side rice     þam ðær selra wæs.     (2196-9)

[In that nation the land was inherited by both together, the soil, the
hereditary right, the broad kingdom – though more to the one there
who was of higher rank.]

Vagueness like that might breed murder in Denmark, but only harmony
among the Hrethlings. And though Hygelac is dead two lines later, it is
not because he was wrong about his relations.

It takes more than just misfortune to generate irony. One might add as
a final reflection that literary irony arises when a reader knows more than a
character who does not know enough. Neither of these conditions is well
fulfilled in the last thousand lines of *Beowulf*. To begin with, though the
proportion of allusive material is in this section very high (almost a
third) it is overwhelmingly historical and retrospective, about matters
known to the characters as well as the readers. Of course Beowulf
himself 'did not know by what means his separation from the world
would come about' (3067-8), while the poet has told us three times
between lines 2310 and 2343 that he and the dragon will kill each other.
Still, he seems to have a shrewd idea. 'His mind was sad' before he fought
the dragon, and after being bitten 'he knew well' that the wound was
mortal. This increased awareness now makes Beowulf unsuitable as a
victim of irony. Furthermore the long experience he has had (and which
he shares with those evident projections of the poet's mind, the Last
Survivor and the Messenger) makes him something of an ironist himself.
He knows how unexpected things can be, and gives as an example the
history of his own three uncles:

> 'Wæs þam yldestan     ungedefelice
> mæges dædum     morþorbed stred,
> syððan hyne Hæðcyn     of hornbogan,
> his freawine     flane geswencte,
> miste mercelses     ond his mæg ofscet,
> broðor oðerne     blodigan gare.'     (2435-40)

[For the eldest a death-bed was unfittingly prepared by a kinsman's
deeds, when Hæthcyn wounded him, his lord, with an arrow from a

horn-bow; he missed the mark and shot his kinsman, one brother
another with a bloody dart.]

'Unfittingly' in that translation is the suggestion of Klaeber's glossary;
but one can see that 'ironically' would fit just as well. Beowulf by this
time has achieved very near equal status with the poet as a truth-speaker.
One could say that he is even raised to superiority by the fact that
perceptions of irony do not daunt him. Though he seems to identify
momentarily with old men reduced to impotence by the son-snatching
twists of fate, in the end he rises to his feet and advances, resolution
undimmed by sad experience. It is hard at this moment to find a chink in
his armour of sober perception, and though later on his belief in the
utility of treasure provides a rather doubtful one, one ought to recognize
at the very least that the balance has changed. The hero's progress is
towards weakness and death, but away from irony and ignorance; near
the centre, too, there is a peaceful and happy state of equilibrium.

## The heathens and the monsters

None of the foregoing explains why Beowulf is a poem about monsters.
Maybe the reason is beyond intellectual grasp: it was a fashion, it was a
tale the poet knew, he just happened to like dragons. However, critics are
reluctant to see no reflection in the story's simple kernel of the attractive
complexities of the surrounding 'interlace'; there are, accordingly, many
variations on the view that the monsters, for all their strongly realized
inner life, are in some way 'symbolic'. Grendel represents death, or
troublemaking, or the body of Satan; the dragon is Leviathan, war,
revenge, the heroic system. The ubiquity of the monsters, the feeling
that in the Beowulfian world one will come along if you only wait long
enough, provokes such rationalizations inevitably. Yet no particular
form of words remains satisfying for long – no doubt because they all
ask us to believe that the poet began with an abstraction to which he
added the flesh and bones of his story, a process which seems even more
alien to him than to most creative writers. Still, the heart of the matter
remains the poet's original conception; and here the monsters do
possibly offer a clue.

   A striking fact about Grendel is that he presents a problem of taxo-
nomy. He is a *þyrs* and an *eoten* – a member, then, of those races of
non-human intelligent beings (like the elves or *ylfe* of line 112) which
figure in pagan Scandinavian mythology. In a Christian cosmos, however, non-human intelligent beings have no secure place, preachers
traditionally explaining them as either devils, or spiritual beings of some

other kind, or ghosts, or of course figments of the imagination.[8] The
*ylfe* of line 112 are accordingly flanked on one side by the *eotenas* of pre-
Christian bogeyland, but on the other by *orcneas* or 'demon corpses', a
conception much easier to fit into the Christian scheme. In any case that
whole passage (102–14) explains that all these beings are actually the
descendants of Cain, equated in learned legend with the 'giants' of
Genesis and destroyed (not very permanently) in the Flood. Logically,
then, Grendel must be a man, and indeed the poet repeatedly calls him
*wer, rinc, guma, maga*, all normal terms for 'man' or 'warrior'. On the
other hand he also calls him *gæst* [spirit] and *feond*, either 'fiend' or
'enemy', but in phrases like *feond on helle* almost inevitably the former.
Epithets like 'enemy of mankind', 'God's adversary', 'prisoner of hell'
bring Grendel even closer conceptually to the devil. And yet he has a soul
and will be judged at Doomsday, two facts which again make him a child
of Adam. All this looks, frankly, like the confusion born of cultural
discrepancy. Yet we should note that the poet can perfectly well think of
phrases which leave the monster/man/devil problem to one side –
'wight', 'march-stepper', 'death-shadow', 'shadow-walker' and so on –
while he actually highlights his difficulties in the thirteen lines mentioned
already, as in Hrothgar's careful statement that one monster is *'idese
onlicnes'* [shaped like a woman], the other *'on weres wæstmum'* [in the form
of a man].[9] Perhaps the poet recognized the problem, but did not *bother*
to solve it.

Perhaps he did the same thing with his heroes. Were they pagan or
Christian? It has already been said that they were in history and outside
the poem definitely pagan, that the poet knew this and said so once, in
line 179. But he never says it again. The word *hæþen* occurs five times
after line 179, but one of these instances is a revealing scribal error, at line
1983, right in the poem's 'warm centre', as Hygd passes the ale-cup
*hæðnum to handa* [to the hands of the heathens]. Almost all editors have
rejected this reading. It is terribly jarring, for just then the Geats are
behaving as mildly and humbly as ever they can, and is most untypical –
a mistake for *hæleðum* [heroes], suggests Klaeber. The scribe, however,
was in a way more reasonable than the poet. Beowulf and Hygelac *were*
heathens, of course. The point is that the poet will not say so. *Hæþen* is
a word he reserves for monsters: Grendel is a 'heathen warrior' with a
'heathen soul', while the dragon, though animal itself, guards and is
defined by its 'heathen gold'.

The suggestion being made is that these two radical ambiguities are

[8] See C. S. Lewis, *The Discarded Image* (Cambridge, 1964), ch. 6.
[9] Tolkien, *op. cit.*, considers 'Grendel's Titles' in an appendix.

connected. The poet had one problem in deciding the nature of monsters. Along with it he had the problem of 'righteous pagans'. Could such creatures exist – people, that is, who had never been offered the means of salvation (Bible and baptism), but who nevertheless acted charitably and properly? The maxim *extra ecclesiam nulla salvatio* [no salvation outside the Church] said 'no', common experience said 'yes'. The history of compromise between the two positions is a long one.[10] However, it is precisely in places like Anglo-Saxon England (where Christian converts might have dead, loved, pagan parents) that the pressure for compromise was fiercest. It may be no accident that the first, optimistic account of the salvation of the pagan Trajan through the tears of Gregory, 'apostle of the English', comes in a book written by a monk of Whitby around AD 710 (and called in question by stricter Christians ever since).[11] In any case it must be clear that a scheme which damned Beowulf and Wealhtheow indiscriminately with Unferth and Heremod could have had little appeal except to spiritual sadists or men of weak imagination. The poet, then, decided to upgrade his heroes to religious neutrality. One way of doing so was to create an image of 'heathenness' from which they were clearly separate – and that is why *Beowulf* is a poem about monsters! This effect was further heightened by the uncertainty round Grendel, for if he were just a *þyrs* Beowulf would lose the credit of doing God's work in killing His adversary, while if he were entirely devil his natural antagonist would be a saint. There are two taxonomic compromises in the poem, but the one is generated by the other.

It may be objected either that this reeks of heresy, or that it makes the poem rest on a double evasion. The poet's voice is, however, often evasive, recognizing the limits of knowledge. No one knows who 'those' were who sent Scyld out on his fateful journey and then took him back again; they cannot have been God, but they hardly seem to be men. No one knows for sure what Sigemund did, either, on his campaigns against the monsters. But these suggestions of a world larger than men's 'middle-earth' can suggest humility rather than heresy, as can the careful, not-to-be-disentangled interweaving of pagan and Christian motifs in Beowulf's last three death-speeches. Salvation is after all God's affair. The poet does the best he can for his heroes by eliminating from their world slaves, sacrifices, incest, all the immediately repulsive accompaniments of

[10] See *Dictionnaire de Théologie Catholique*, ed. A. Vacant and E. Mangenot (15 vols, Paris, 1903–46), s.v. 'Infidèles, salut des', vol. 7, 1726–930.

[11] See *The Earliest Life of Gregory the Great*, ed. and trans. B. Colgrave (Lawrence Ka., 1968), pp. 161–3.

paganism. But he will not go so far as to say, untruthfully, that they were really Christians. At line 1865 it is Hrothgar who asserts that the Danes and Geats are 'in every respect guiltless, in the ancient fashion' [*æghwæs untæle ealde wisan*], but the statement is not openly ratified. What the poet has done is to create a universe which is lifelike, consistent, a model for emulation, and one seen through a film of antique nostalgia; but which remains at the same time a world the poet and all his contemporaries could properly thank their God they did not live in.

# 4. Poetry and its Functions

*Compounds, variations, formulas*

All literary effects depend finally on <u>words</u>, and it is the last responsibility of the *Beowulf* critic to examine the way the poet uses them. That is not the same, though, as agreeing with A. G. Brodeur that 'what concerns us is the quality of his work as poetry'.[1] For this last formulation implies several of the deepest-rooted and least-challenged pieties of modern criticism – that poetry is something above analysis, a true goal beyond mean considerations of utility, permanent and universal and speaking directly to the reader's heart. Certainly the author of *Beowulf* put a high valuation on his craft. On the other hand he was not above connecting it with horse-racing (lines 853 ff.). There is no sign in his work of the superstitious veneration for poetry which we have learnt from Romanticism and its successors.

It is accordingly not disrespectful to remark on one of the sorest and least-probed points of Beowulfian style – its casual way with compound words. Consider the powerful and successful section at the end of the Grendel-fight, lines 809–36. As the monster disappears into death and darkness, the poet remarks of Beowulf:

> Nihtweorce gefeh,
> ellenmærþum.   Hæfde East-Denum
> Geatmecga leod   gilp gelæsted . . .          (827–9)

[He rejoiced in his night's work, the fame his courage won. The man of the Geats had fulfilled his boast to the East-Danes.]

Why '*East*-Danes'? The same people were 'North-Danes' forty lines before (783), 'South-Danes' before that (463), and 'West-Danes' on Beowulf's arrival (383). They have been 'Spear-Danes' and 'Ring-Danes' and 'Bright-Danes' too, but at least you can be all those things together, while to most people 'east' definitely precludes 'west', as 'north' does 'south'. Of course *East* has been put into line 828 *only* to make the

[1] A. G. Brodeur, *The Art of Beowulf* (Berkeley and Los Angeles, 1959), p. 3.

necessary alliteration with *ellen*. That is the only reason for many of the
poem's other compound forms, and for many more it is the strongest
reason. A few lines above *East-Denum* the poet says that Grendel knew
his end had come, *dogera dægrim*. This phrase is entirely tautologous,
meaning literally 'the day-number of his days'. A more sensible word
would be *dogorgerim* (used at line 2728) but in line 823 that would not
scan. *Dæg* is thrown in, then, to make up the weight. One could balk at
line 820 as well, when Grendel has to escape, *feorhseoc fleon under fen-*
*hleoðu* [flee life-sick under fen-slopes]. This is a good line, in grim
contrast with the futile purpose of the next phrase, 'to seek a joyless
dwelling'. But '*fen*-slopes'? A *hlið* is something steep, cliff or hillside or
even wall. Fens, however, are flat. It is hard to resist the thought that the
poet wanted a compound word which would scan, imply inaccessibility,
and above all alliterate on *f*; he created *fenhleoðu*, then, by a kind of
double analogy with the *misthleoðu* [misty slopes] of line 710 and the
*fenfreoðu* [fenfastnesses] of 851. The word sounds all right, but it is not
meant to stand close examination.

This is not to say that the *Beowulf* poet *never* used words imaginatively.
But he did accept an element of redundance and tautology as part of
his style (just as he saw no sin in heroes drinking). Compounds like
*heal-reced* and *heal-ærn* (they both mean 'hall-building' or even 'hall-
hall') are then neither tributes to the vividness of his imagination –
though they form part of Professor Brodeur's statistics of originality –
nor signs of intellectual barrenness. They are, like the poet's many
indistinguishable synonyms, simply functional; and their function is to
create metric or alliterative pattern.

It can hardly be a coincidence that the poem's next most evident
feature of style also has clear utility. This is 'variation', and examples of
it are everywhere. The lines just quoted about Beowulf fulfilling his
boast continue:

> swylce oncyþðe       ealle gebette,
> inwidsorge,       þe hie ær drugon
> ond for þreanydum       þolian scoldon,
> torn unlytel.                                     (830–33)

[Also cured all their distress, the sorrow and the malice they had
endured and in painful necessity had had to endure, no little grief.]

Anyone can see that *inwidsorge* and *torn* are both 'variations' of the idea
first expressed in *oncyþðe*, while the whole of line 832 is an expansion of
*þe hie ær drugon* just before; anyone can see, too, that the poet is enjoying
the cumulative roll of vanished miseries, with the sharp litotes of *unlytel*

at the end. Just the same, the 'variations' in *Beowulf* keep on arriving even when their necessity is less than evident (for example in lines 350–55). What they do is help the poet 'change step', that is, move from one essential idea to the next without losing alliteration. In this section, for instance, the poet's final and clearly deliberate stroke is to end with the image of Beowulf showing his grisly trophy, Grendel's arm, to the watching men. *Þæt wæs tacen sweotol*, he says with enthusiastic under-understatement, 'it was a clear indication, once, bold in battle, he laid down the hand, the arm and shoulder – there was Grendel's grip all together – laid it down beneath the vaulted roof' (833–6). The *tacen*, we can see, is a vital part of the section's narrative structure; but its entry has been much eased by the semantically redundant use of *torn*.

Having got so far, one can hardly avoid the concept of 'orality'. Does the poet's functionalism not suggest a man who will have to recite his poem to listeners who cannot be expected to ponder over every single word he says? Could it not even imply a man himself illiterate who never so much as imagined the scrupulous concepts of literary criticism? These questions (and several others) have in recent years been almost literally bedevilled by the discovery of a third stylistic feature of *Beowulf* – the formula, sometimes called the oral-formula. The facts behind this phrase can be briefly stated.[2] Through the whole of *Beowulf* about one half line in six will be repeated more or less exactly elsewhere in the poem: examples include *hine fyrwyt bræc*, already discussed, or in the lines just quoted *ellenmærþum* and *þe hie ær drugon*. Very many more will be repeated with slight (or great) changes: thus *nihtweorce gefeh* (827) is at least rather like *secg weorce gefeh* (1569), while *ond for þreanydum* (832) is virtually identical with *ac for preanedlan* (2223). Any search for repetitions in *Beowulf* uncovers vast but not easily organized sets of resem-blances; and these once more offer radical challenge to concepts of originality, precision, the poetic mind. Thus to many the epithet *nacod niðdraca* in line 2273 seems beautifully calculated to evoke the monster's obscenely and unnaturally leathery hide, the famous armour-plating of the longworm. On the other hand the poet alliterates *nið* and *nacod* elsewhere, in line 2585, where he is talking about swords, and he has a whole range of similar phrases for the dragon, some of them ('dangerous fire-dragon', 'terrible earth-dragon') no more tightly appropriate than Grendel's *fenhleoðu*. You can, in short, regard the brilliant stroke as one more accidental overlap of two repetitive systems; the formulas turn out

[2] For a full account, including explanations of 'one half line in six' and 'more or less exactly', see A. C. Watts, *The Lyre and the Harp* (New Haven and London, 1969), especially appendix B, pp. 227–65.

as functional as the compounds and the variations, and as artistically neutral. Some critics welcome these implications as a gain in precision. To others the whole line of thought acts as intolerable provocation to their most cherished notions of individual art.

The problem is ours, not the poet's. Once again the overwhelming temptation for modern readers is to bring to the poem preconceived ideas of beauty and worth, to insist on praising it for what we have already decided is praiseworthy. *Beowulf* lends itself to these arguments, as it does to symbolic interpretations, ironic interpretations, even the neo-classic interpretations of days gone by. That does not make any of them right. Furthermore we must fear that while we pursue sterile contro-versies of art versus accident and oral versus literate, we are shirking the real problem, which is to see what the poet would himself have found stylistically admirable. In pursuing this objective, probably the most use-ful thing we can do with compounds, variations and formulas is jettison them; and with them our quasi-autobiographical curiosity about mode of composition. The latter cannot be satisfied. As for the features of style already discussed, they *are* prominent and they *do* tell us something, but the most useful thing they tell us is that for the underlying charm and power of the poem – as distinct from minor local lapses or neatnesses – we shall have to look elsewhere. The style of *Beowulf* is clearly functional. But we want to know what aim these functions serve.

## Fragmentation and control

One can make a start here by considering once more the end of the Grendel fight. Here if anywhere the poet is deliberately manipulating his audience. From the start of the struggle he has been insisting that Beowulf's will is unbreakable, and so is his grip. Grendel 'could not get away' (754), he 'knew his fingers held in the fierce one's grip' (764–5); as for Beowulf, he 'held him firmly' (788), 'not for anything would he let the evil visitor escape alive' (791–2). So how does Grendel manage to flee to the fens? At the crucial moment the poet evades us, slipping from the physical bursting of bones in line 818 to the abstraction of *guðhreð*, success and glory in 819. The answer is held in suspense for fifteen lines. *Then* the poet says it was 'a clear sign' [*tacen sweotol*] when Beowulf laid down the hand and arm and shoulder 'beneath the vaulted roof'. The hero's grip has not weakened, we see; instead it was the monster's fear which proved stronger than his flesh.

I have commented elsewhere on the poet's love of constructions which tell us first about results and only second about their causes,[3] but the

---

[3] Shippey, *Old English Verse*, pp. 36–8.

immediate point here is the strongly *visual* quality of the poet's rhetoric. One can hardly avoid saying that he 'cuts' from the mighty wound to Grendel fleeing dimly into the night, that at the end he 'narrows focus' to the arm 'framed' by the vaulted roof. Of course all these words are cinematic, and so anachronisms. Still, they can remind us that the poet obviously did not mean his words to stay on the page, but to stimulate mental images. Sometimes he directs his audience to visualize, using words like *ȝþgesene*: 'On the bench there over each prince you could easily have seen. . . .' More often he gives them something to look at, and characters inside the poem looking at it. The Danes pursuing Grendel's mother come upon Æschere's head with exactly the same shock as those in Heorot staring at Grendel's arm, and the poet stops to let them (and us) drink it in: *Folc to sægon*, he prompts (1422), 'the people looked at it'. Two hundred lines later it is Grendel's head which appears on the floor of Heorot within a frame of spectators:

> Þa wæs be feaxe    on flet boren
> Grendles heafod,    þær guman druncon,
> egeslic for eorlum    ond þære idese mid,
> wliteseon wrætlic;    weras on sawon.    (1647–50)

[Then Grendel's head was carried by its hair on to the floor where the men were drinking, a terrible thing for the warriors and the woman with them, a splendid and beautiful sight; the men looked at it.]

In between Beowulf has (quite redundantly) asked the Danes to visualize Hygelac receiving the news of his death: 'Then the lord of the Geats can realize, the son of Hrethel see, when he stares at the treasure [*þonne he on þæt sinc starað*] that I found a good divider of rings . . .' (1484–7). And when the slave makes off with the dragon's cup, he shows it to his master:

>                frea sceawode
> fira fyrngeweorc    forman siðe.    (2285–6)

[For the first time the lord looked at the ancient work of men.]

Silent vision is an important part of the poet's craft; he manufactures occasions for it. That is why we have the rapid and much-admired interchange of external and internal views as Grendel bears down on Heorot (702–27). That is equally why, after Beowulf has killed Grendel's mother in the submarine hall, the poet cannot resist switching to Hrothgar and the others fathoms above, standing and watching the blood spread in the water. Silently the Danes ride home. As silently the

Geats sit and stare at the mere, wishing hopelessly that they could 'see their lord himself'. But the sight to which the poet redirects us is the giant sword melting like an icicle in Grendel's blood. The emotional contrasts are presented entirely visually.

Of course this makes excellent sense as a mode of narration for audiences not yet surfeited by television. What is less commonly realized, however, is how far down the stylistic scale this quality of manipulated vision goes. It is something which (unlike compound words and formulas) resists quantification. Nevertheless, the most powerful consistent feature of Beowulfian style is what may be called its 'epic brokenness' – the poet's determination not to let successive sentences resemble each other syntactically or describe events from the same point of view.

Some examples of this have already been cited. We are switched in lines 818–19 from physical 'joints' to abstract 'glory'; in line 825 we turn from simple past to pluperfect, as the poet invites us to consider all the courage and misery that preceded this turn of events; and in lines 827–8 we get a neat 'double perspective' in time as Beowulf rejoices simultaneously over what he has done (*nihtweorce*) and what he will get (*ellenmærþum*). More generally we can see that the whole of this fight has been described in a way peripherally, with attention being repeatedly directed away from the centre to the effects that that centre produces – the echoing hall, the smashed benches, the gallant but ineffective crowd of Geats, outside them the Danes listening in horror to the screams of Grendel, 'God's adversary singing a terror-song . . . the captive of hell lamenting his pain'. Perhaps most remarkable, though, is the poet's occasional approach to 'stream of consciousness', as for instance in his account of Ongentheow, the grim old Swedish king, falling back in sullen anger before the unexpected Geatish *revanche*. In lines 2949–57 the poet, unusually, allows this character to remain the syntactic subject of five main verbs in succession: he 'went away . . . turned back; he had heard of the warfare of Hygelac, the proud man's battle-skill; he had no faith in resistance, in beating off the seamen, defending from the invaders his treasure, wife and children; again he turned away, old man beneath the earth-wall.' One sees how discontinuous even this 'stream' is, as the strongly implied conjunctions like 'because' and 'so' are omitted, as new facts like the rampart and Ongentheow's children emerge from each new clause. There are few passages in *Beowulf* of more direct narrative than this, and yet even here one sees the love of proceeding by a series of minor shocks – of keeping reader or listener from reaching any easy sense of predictability, while letting him see, feel, remember, conclude only those exact things which the narrator intends.

This too could be explained, incidentally, as one more accident of alliterative convention. In line 815 we have a typically sudden leap from emotion to fact, one of the poem's innumerable 'changes of angle':

                      wæs gehwæþer oðrum
lifigende lað.    Licsar gebad
atol aglæca.                        (814–16)

[Each was to the other hateful while he lived. The dreadful monster received a body wound.]

Is it coincidence, though, that in the poem *lif* and *lic* alliterate together five more times? There is an obvious reason why they should, since they mean something similar, are easily related: in line 2571 Beowulf's shield fails to protect 'life and body' [*life ond lice*], in line 2743 he says he must die, 'life go from body' [*lif of lice*]. But in 815 this semantic connection has become a discontinuity, separating different sentences. Is this (like *fenhleoðu* or *nacod niðdraca*) another compulsive prompting from the traditional vocabulary? Maybe so. However, the observation hardly matters. If one studies compounds and formulas in *Beowulf*, one can often feel that the poet's attention has wandered. When it comes to modes of revelation and concealment, however, his delight and involvement are unmistakable. Certainly he snaps up the opportunities created by traditional pairs like *lif* and *lic* or *fyr* and *flod*, and readers used to the explanatory smoothness of modern prose may feel that, for him, any excuse to change his viewpoint will do. Still, on this level his attention never wavers; there is nothing in the poem as banal visually as 'East-Danes' is verbally. The poet's style is fragmented, but his voice projects control.

### Stasis, pleonasm, cumulation

It is indeed typical of the poem to develop strength from what would by orthodox literary canons be weakness. Its characters do not develop or change. Admittedly Beowulf himself is presented first as young and then as old, and it has been shown how vital to the poem this final sense of age is.[4] However, it is also true to say that the *way* this complex feeling is produced verbally is by simple combination of epithets once reserved for Hrothgar, the old and passive king (*se wisa, frod cyning, þone gomelan*), with others which remind us that the hero is still in heart what he was (*se goda, oretta, heard under helme*). What is moving is not awareness of

---

[4] By John C. Pope, 'Beowulf's Old Age', in *Philological Essays in Honour of H. D. Merritt*, ed. J. L. Rosier (The Hague and Paris, 1970), pp. 55–64.

change, but juxtaposition of fixed purpose with changed circumstance.
'When I was young I did many battles', says Beowulf, as if to himself:

>                          'gyt ic wylle,
>     frod folces weard          fæhðe secan,
>     mærðu fremman. . . .'                          (2512–14)

[Once more I will, old guardian of the people, seek out violence, do
famous deeds.]

Never before has he been *frod folces weard;* but *fæhðe* and *mærðu* have
been his goals a dozen times already. Even this case, then, supports the
assertion that Beowulfian characters do not change their true nature,
though indeed this may be progressively revealed.

Sometimes the result is a peculiar inappositeness. Beowulf says of
Hrothgar (2107) *'hwilum hildedeor hearpan grette'* [sometimes, bold in
battle, he touched the harp]. But Hrothgar is no longer *hildedeor,* and
even if he were, it would have nothing to do with his harping. Similarly,
as Unferth lends Beowulf his sword, the poet remarks contemptuously
that 'the son of Ecglaf surely forgot, mighty in strength [*eafoþes cræftig*]
what he had said before, drunk with wine, now he lent his weapon to a
better swordsman' (1465–8). *Eafoþes cræftig?* We feel the phrase ought to
continue the criticism, and so translators tend to render it by some such
word as 'strapping' (which implies disapproval). Alternatively the phrase
can be explained as 'ironic'. But the fact is that both the style and the
ideology of the poem continue to use honorifics up to the moment
(as with the ten cowards after line 2846) when they are formally
removed. There are occasions when this inflexibility becomes a definite
asset.

As Beowulf and Hrothgar part, for instance, the old king breaks down,
weeping at the thought that they will never meet again. 'Locked in the
bonds of his heart', observes the poet, 'a gloomy longing for the man
he loved burnt in his blood' (1878–80). But Beowulf simply walks
away:

>                          Him Beowulf þanan,
>     guðrinc goldwlanc          græsmoldan træd
>     since hremig;          sægenga bad
>     agendfrean,     se þe on ancre rad.          (1880–83)

[Away from him the gold-proud war-man trod the grassy turf,
exulting in treasure; the sea-crosser which rode at anchor was waiting
for its lord.]

Insensitivity? The vicious pride of youth? Without the expectations of the epic style we might think so. But as it is, the shining figure trampling the grass conveys something exhilarating, the more so for the grief and foreboding which surround him. We know Beowulf is going to die; he is separated from any possible audience of the poem by a great gap of time; and yet for a moment he exists in sharp focus down the tunnel of years, real and happy and triumphant. Poetry has made him immortal. And an element in that process is the way that despair sloughs off him, leaving his character unmarked. We see the same movement at the start of the poem's last section, as the Geats turn from grief to action: 'For him then the people of the Geats prepared a pyre on earth, no mean one' (3137-8). They are as correct in their silence as was Beowulf himself, confronted with the beast his men tugged from the monsters' mere: 'The men gazed at the terrible stranger. Beowulf prepared himself in warriors' equipment, nothing did he care for life . . .'(1440-42). In a hard world, we might reflect, emotional stasis could be as much of a positive as sensitivity.

Line 3138, however, displays a further potential weakness of epic style in its pleonasm: the phrase *on eorðan* is redundant, for where else would you build a pyre if not on the ground? Throwing in the odd 'on earth' or 'under heaven' is a common device of the Anglo-Saxon poet under stress, and the author of *Beowulf* does not scorn it. In his poem, though, pleonasm can work; it is indeed the first stylistic device we should become aware of. As early as line 13 a child is born to Scyld, *geong in geardum* [young in the yards]. Once Scyld is dead this son rules: *Ða wæs on burgum Beowulf Scyldinga* [then in the towns was Beowulf the Scylding]. *His* son was 'the high Healfdene', and to him in turn four children *in woruld wocun* [woke into the world]. Before long it is the other Beowulf, the poem's hero, who is using the same locution, for he says his father is dead and gone, *'gamol of geardum'* [old man from the yards], counterbalancing the Danish Beowulf who was born *geong in geardum* at the start, paralleling Scyld himself who 'went elsewhere' in death, *aldor of earde* [as a chief from the earth]. This cluster of similar phrases works insidiously and powerfully, along with the repeated images of coming, waking up, travelling out, to create a picture of the common habitations, the homelands, the *geardas*, set in space against the universe that surrounds them and in time against the mystery of death. To these forces men oppose their fleeting happiness, their children, their social rituals of memory and inheritance. The composite image becomes deeply embedded in the poem as a whole, ready to be restimulated positively by the mention of home or inheritance (see lines 693, 912, 1127; 1960 ff., 2470 ff., 2623 ff.), or negatively by the rumour of great and ominous forces

just outside the light – those for instance who sent out Scyld on his
journey, *ænne ofer yðe, umborwesende* [alone over seas, being a child], and
who take back his treasure-piled body in the end:

> Men ne cunnon
> secgan to soðe,      selerædende,
> hæleð under heofenum,      hwa þæm hlæste onfeng.   (50–52)

[Men cannot say for sure, hall-councillors, heroes under heavens, who
received that cargo.]

The heroes are heroes, one might say, because they are 'under heavens'
and know so little; the phrase is resonantly appropriate. It is not destroyed
if one remarks that it is also an evident cliché which can (as in line 505)
be used entirely mechanically.

The images of pleonasm work in fact as spatial counterparts to the
rhythms of temporal opposition which the poet again extracts from
formula and elevates to principle – the circle of sadness after joy and joy
after sadness once more. Hrothgar explains this most openly in his
long 'disguised narrator' speech of lines 1700–1784, whose climax is
direct appeal to Beowulf (and through him to us). Look at me, says
Hrothgar, I was confident once, I ruled the Ring-Danes 'beneath the
clouds'.

> 'Hwæt, me þæs on eþle      edwenden cwom,
> gyrn æfter gomene,      seoþðan Grendel wearð,
> ealdgewinna,      ingenga min.'                        (1774–6)

[To me in my home came a change from this, grief after pleasure, once
Grendel, old enemy, became my invader.]

We see the use of *on eþle* in 1774, the syntactic delay of *scopðan* in 1775,
both devices already mentioned. Between them, though, lies the
fierce reversal of *gyrn æfter gomene*. To this pattern the poet has drawn our
attention before – *swylt æfter synnum* in 1255, *æfter wea . . . wyrp* in 909,
*æfter þam wælræse willa* in 824 [death after sins, recovery after woe, desire
after deadly battle]. He makes the rhythm emblematic in line 1008 as
Grendel 'sleeps after banquet', and as the Danish warriors are found
'sleeping after banquet' in line 119, only to be betrayed by sleep to
Grendel. The pattern leads readily to the repetitions of 'they knew not
sorrow, the fortune of men' in 119–20, and 'they knew not fate, grim
destiny' a thousand lines later. It finds its way from moralizing to
description when the Danes wake and find their dead in line 128: 'Then
was after banquet lamentation raised' [*wop æfter wiste*]; and into direct

speech when Hrothgar tells Beowulf: 'Don't ask after joy; sorrow is renewed' [*sorh æfter sælum*]. As often, indeed, the poet and his characters turn out indistinguishable. Their shared image of human precariousness finds multiple but consistent expression.

There is little point, finally, in arguing whether the poet was or was not conscious of these repeated structures. What matters is that even if he employed them consciously, he did so un*self*consciously. His tricks of rhetoric often have learned names – pleonasm, paronomasia, essential hypotaxis. They remain, however, familiar parts of English speech; anyone who says 'brain versus brawn' or 'I'll love you and leave you' is using paronomasia as surely as the *Beowulf* poet opposing *lof* to *lif* or *wæl* to *willa*. Of course clichés do not spontaneously generate poetry. Nevertheless, the point remains: the stylistic power of *Beowulf* depends not on close fit of words to scenes but on bold use of familiar phrasing. The poet's art, like his philosophy, is rooted in commonplace.

## The gnomic voice

The core of this involvement with truth and truism is found in the poem's many maxims. These have fallen predictably foul of modern critical taste, which tends to ignore them, apologize for them, or else (as with compound words) to look for some originality underlying their evidently shared and communal nature. The most justifiable reason for this dislike is the fact that many Beowulfian maxims, in strict logic, mean nothing. 'God can easily restrain the evil-doer from his deeds', says Hrothgar at lines 478–9, and the very wording of the phrase protects it from disproof. Yes, God *can*. But is He going to? Beowulf's victory in fact shows that He was, and Hrothgar accordingly repeats the gist of his 'sentence' (930–31). But even if Beowulf had lost, the maxim would remain potentially and forever true. Still, what use is an inherently uncheckable statement? One might ask the same of Beowulf's own *Spruch* – a popular one, repeated maybe five centuries later in the Old Norse *Fóstbrœðra saga*, chapter 23 – that 'Fate often spares the undoomed man, as long as his courage holds'. In this one can translate *wyrd* and *unfægne* all sorts of ways, but two near-contradictory things are still being said: (a) not even Fate will save a man whose courage does *not* hold (b) the bravest of man will die if he is *fæg*. Keep fighting, then; it may be no use! As a predictor, the statement is as useless as Hrothgar's, its semantic emptiness only surpassed by Beowulf's later, 'Things always go as they must' [*Gæð a wyrd swa hio scel*], a statement as undeniable as inscrutable. Still, it is no use thinking that this vice is confined to characters speaking under stress. The poet very nearly duplicates all four of the maxims just mentioned with the conclusion he draws from the dragon-thief's escape:

> Swa mæg unfæge     eaðe gedigan
> wean ond wræcsið     se ðe Waldendes
> hyldo gehealdeþ!                                    (2291–3)

[So a man who is not doomed can easily survive sorrow and exile, if he keeps God's favour.]

But why should the dragon-thief be in God's good books? Maybe he committed the theft inadvertently, but he shows little desire to make up for it, as we see from lines 2406–10. Evidently there is something compulsive about this voicing of gnomic statements; and the compulsion lies on the poet as well as the characters.

The key to these difficulties lies in the observation made once already, that proverbs are not merely linguistic phenomena; they also tell you what you may or may not accept as true. As such their importance is not gauged by their logic, and they communicate (to those who understand them) with supra-verbal directness. Actually we realize quite well that Hrothgar's early statements mean 'I will not give way to despair', Beowulf's 'I will feel no fear'. Gnomes often contain an element of defiance against mere physical fact. So, when Beowulf says (1386–7), 'Each one of us must endure an end of life in this world', he is asserting not mortality but its opposite – that since death is sure we should take no notice of it. And though this may not be immediately logical, we cannot say that it makes no sense! Further, the maxims are often exercises in self-definition, telling you exactly what people ought to be. When Wiglaf says that 'for every warrior [eorla gehwylcum] death is better than a life of shame', he is also saying that a man who prefers death to shame is an eorl. When Beowulf reports that Hrethel left his children land and homestead 'as an honest man does' [swa deð eadig mon], he also implies that honest men own property. These conclusions may be unpalatable, and they are frequently false as well, but that once more does not matter. What matters is that social ideals have been created and passed on, propriety equated unforgettably with reality.

As I have said elsewhere,[5] it can be difficult even on the levels of grammar to distinguish in *Beowulf* between statements and maxims, between what ought to be and what is. But this uncertainty is strength

---

[5] Shippey, 'Maxims in Old English Narrative: Literary Art or Traditional Wisdom?', in *Oral Tradition, Literary Tradition: A Symposium*, ed. H. Bekker-Nielsen *et al.* (Odense, 1977), pp. 28–46.

not weakness. It gives the poem a final element of solidarity, assuring readers or listeners that they and the poet and the characters are in essentials on the same side, sharing the same assumptions. Of course, by the accidents of history, we no longer *do* share the same assumptions (and that is why the maxims so often create incomprehension or alarm). That does not mean the poem has lost its pull. We have to work harder at recovering the sense of what is said, and we have to do it while suspending some of our own learnt codifications; on the other hand a familiar element still persists, while there is also a glamour of strangeness and intellectual difficulty to compensate (quite unfairly) the equal unfairness of lost heritage. The verve of some of the poet's claims comes over unabated, as when Beowulf throws down his useless sword to an accompanying authorial cheer:

> Swa sceal man don,
> þonne he æt guðe     gegan þenceð
> longsumne lof;     na ymb his lif cearað.     (1534-6)

[So must a man do, when he means to gain lasting glory in battle; life is not what he thinks about.]

So does occasional regret:

> Sinc eaðe mæg,
> gold on grunde     gumcynnes gehwone
> oferhigian,     hyde se ðe wylle!     (2764-6)

[Hide it who will, treasure can easily, gold in the ground, overmaster any of the race of men.]

And yet that particular 'sentence' (third and last of the poet's *eaðe mæg* set) may serve to remind us once more of the dangers of appreciating this unfamiliar style. The pleonastic variation of *gold on grunde* is here extremely powerful, hinting at the strange charm above all of *buried* treasure, arousing a vestige of the dangerous lust it describes. And yet *gold on grunde* in a sense means no more than *sinc*, existing primarily to keep alliteration going. To dwell on it would be mistaken. In the same way the maxim as a whole is extremely powerful, suggesting the entrapment of Beowulf and Wiglaf as well by their all too human instinct for greed. But does it imply exactly that? The poet likes maxims too much to leave them out. Sometimes he puts them in, one feels, just because he thinks them true, not because he thinks they are to be applied to their immediate context. One has only to look at lines 1002 ff. to see how sententiousness could sweep over him. So over-close attention to maxims may be as wrong as complete distaste for them; in the same way as precise attention to the meaning of every single Beowulfian word often exposes the poet in shift or expediency.

Above all the style of *Beowulf* depends on pace, on visualization, on letting the poet exercise his right to switch from close description to loose reflection. Its aphorisms demand involvement rather than scrutiny, and without this remain mere words, as weak emotionally as factually untrue. Without similar involvement *Beowulf* too would descend to the status of a romance, a tale of long ago. Yet that is not how its creator saw it. Nor, more surprisingly, is that how it continues to be read, translated, paraphrased, and drawn on, even in the to him unimaginable circumstances of the present, a thousand years and as many barriers from the world in which it was composed.

# 5. Afterword

At this point in critical essays one is supposed to present 'conclusions'. However, these ought by now to be obvious; and since I have already so often expressed discontent with the conventions of criticism, I would like finally to abandon them and set down plainly some personal opinions.

To begin with, I think the worst failure of recent *Beowulf* scholarship has been the inability to capitalize on the 'oral-formulaic' initiatives of Milman Parry. His adherents were careless and his opponents conservative, and both saw 'oral' and 'literate' as mutually exclusive. It has recently been pointed out, though, that literate people can live in pre-literate societies, just as illiterates can live in our own.[1] But both minorities have to conform, at least until the stage when (as in most medieval societies) the illiterate majority comes to accept that everything important is written down. At this point the nature of literacy is likely to change; irony, for instance, emerges from inconsistency, as does symbolism from straight description. Professors Bäuml and Spielmann take the argument further in their article on the *Nibelungenlied* cited below. But I can now say no more than that many of the problems of *Beowulf* dissolve if one accepts it as the work of a illiterate man n a pre-literate society – one might say, a sort of Cædmon in reverse.

A further failure of scholarship, in my opinion, has been inability to cope with allegorists. No single allegorical reading of *Beowulf* has ever ousted the others,[2] and yet the urge to produce them remains, unweakened by literal arguments. The trouble is that the human mind is a pattern-producing machine; it even sees shapes in random constellations. Accordingly allegory, like irony, can never be disproved directly. Its true weakness lies in the innumerable details its discoverers are too single-minded to include: Yrmenlaf, the racehorses, the painted shields of the Danes, Beowulf as a seven-year-old taken from his father, the stolen

[1] See F. H. Bäuml and E. Spielmann, 'From Illiteracy to Literacy: Prolegomena to a Study of the *Nibelungenlied*', in *Oral Literature*, ed. J. J. Duggan (Edinburgh, 1975), pp. 62–73.
[2] The most powerful is, however, M. Goldsmith's *The Mode and Meaning of Beowulf* (London, 1970).

bride of Ongentheow, the snapped ribs of Dæghrefn – all that gives the
poem life. Separately all these facts (and hundreds more) can be ignored;
their collective absence from consideration makes moral allegory thin
and sour.

But at the same time I think that the modern preference for multiple
meaning and non-didacticism has also made the poem unnecessarily
difficult, has indeed smothered it in problems. Actually the poet often
tells us what he is writing about – change and the certainty of death and
how to balance pessimism with optimism. When he is not being proverbial he is repeatedly 'proverbious', saying things which sound general
though they happen to be particular. In my opinion a large part of his
meaning is summed up in lines 2188-9 and 2265-6: the former say that
'a change for every misery came to the valiant man', and imply that such
changes always come to *all* valiant men. The latter insist, conversely but
not incompatibly, that 'hateful death has sent away many races of men'
(and will, of course, do the same to many more). Hope for the best, then,
prepare for the worst: traditional advice, but never out of place. To this
one might add that the poet has a further particular aversion, and that is
killing kinsmen, or *morþorbealo maga* (see lines 1079, 2742). His views on
the ethics of warfare were not ours, and I think he accepted social
instability as a fact of life; however, though we may feel it a narrow
moral, he obviously believed blood *ought* to be thicker than water, and
saw the contrast of merely piratical Geats with internecine Swedes and
Danes accordingly.

So the meaning of *Beowulf* is not unusually hard to apprehend. That is
not the same as finding it easy to comprehend. The final observation I
would like to make about the poem is that it is almost implausibly
consistent in minor matters. No one has, to my knowledge, written the
poem's 'syntax of gestures' – people stacking weapons or leaving them
outside, people walking round the hall, drinking in turn, sitting at each
other's feet or standing before their shoulders, people going through
rituals of greeting and parting and donation and boast. Yet this would be
an easy job, would turn out plausible, significant, internally as cohesive
as the royal pedigrees which the poet never bothers to set out but which
all editors neatly reconstruct and transcribe into their introductions.
Could the poet have invented either the dynasties or the behaviour
patterns? And then had the self-restraint to keep them so far from
prominence? I cannot believe it myself. This is not 'realism' but truth:
to put it more exactly, the poet believed he was describing facts, whether
these were mere historical ones or matters still accepted in his own time.
That is why the poem is more than fiction and better than something

just original. To close with one critical heresy more: I do not think the ultimate justification of *Beowulf* is its creator's art, but rather its characters' poise and self-possession and tireless oral propriety. My own image of the anonymous poet resembles Virgil less than it does a bolder and more taciturn Lord Chesterfield.

# Further Reading

This list should be taken in conjunction with the works already cited.

Larry D. Benson, 'The Pagan Coloring of *Beowulf*', in *Old English Poetry*, ed. R. P. Creed (Providence, 1967), pp. 193–213.

A. Bonjour, *The Digressions in Beowulf* (Oxford, 1950).

A. G. Brodeur, *The Art of Beowulf* (Berkeley and Los Angeles, 1959).

N. K. Chadwick, 'The Monsters and Beowulf', in *The Anglo-Saxons*, ed. P. Clemoes (London, 1959), pp. 171–203.

R. W. Chambers, *Beowulf: an Introduction* (3rd edn with supplement by C. L. Wrenn, Cambridge, 1959).

U. Dronke, 'Beowulf and Ragnarok', *Saga-Book of the Viking Society*, vol. 17, part 4 (1969), pp. 302–25.

E. B. Irving Jr, *A Reading of Beowulf* (New Haven and London, 1968).

L. E. Nicholson (ed.), *An Anthology of Beowulf Criticism* (Notre Dame, 1963).

T. A. Shippey, 'The Fairy-Tale Structure of *Beowulf*', *Notes and Queries* n.s. 16 (1969), pp. 2–11.

K. Sisam, *The Structure of Beowulf* (Oxford, 1965).

E. G. Stanley, '*Beowulf*', in *Continuations and Beginnings*, ed. E. G. Stanley (London, 1966,) pp. 104–41.

J. R. R. Tolkien, '*Beowulf*: the Monsters and the Critics', *Proceedings of the British Academy* 22 (1936), pp. 245–95.

D. Whitelock, *The Audience of Beowulf* (Oxford, 1951).

Of the many translations of *Beowulf* available, the best are those of E. Talbot Donaldson (New York, 1966), K. Crossley-Holland (London, 1968), and M. Alexander (Penguin Classics, Harmondsworth, 1973). Howell D. Chickering's 'Dual-Language Edition' (New York, 1977), is also extremely helpful, as are the many texts translated in G. N. Garmonsway and J. Simpson's *Beowulf and its Analogues* (London and New York, 1968).

# Index